AF735090

# FUNDED

# FUNDED

## THE COMPLETE SBA LOAN GUIDE FOR HOTEL OWNERS

*Your Insider's Roadmap to Financing Your Hotel or Motel*

BY THOMAS HARTWELL

Published by Hartwell Labs

www.hartwelllabs.com

First Edition, 2026

ISBN-13 (Ebook): 979-8-9947079-0-6

ISBN-13 (Paperback): 979-8-9947079-1-3



Printed in the United States of America

What's New in This Edition

This edition reflects critical SBA policy changes effective March 1, 2026:

- Citizenship Requirements Updated: Lawful Permanent Residents (Green Card holders) are no longer eligible for SBA loans. Only U.S. Citizens and U.S. Nationals with Principal Residence in the United States may apply. (PN 5000-876441)
- Credit Scoring Changed: The FICO SBSS scoring requirement for 7(a) Small Loans has been discontinued. Lenders now use their own credit analysis processes. (PN 5000-875701)

All affected sections include "(effective March 1, 2026)" markers so you can easily identify current policy.

**This Book Is For You If...**

You're looking at a hotel, motel, or hospitality property and wondering how to finance it. You've been turned down by traditional banks—or you suspect you will be. You have 10-15% to put down, not the 25-35% conventional lenders demand. You want the truth about SBA hotel loans: what qualifies, what doesn't, and how to avoid the mistakes that kill deals. Whether you're a first-time buyer or adding to your portfolio, this guide gives you the insider's roadmap to get funded.

# TABLE OF CONTENTS

CHAPTER 1

# IS SBA FINANCING RIGHT FOR YOUR HOTEL BUSINESS?

You've found the property. A 42-room independent motel off I-95, priced at $1.8 million. The seller accepted your offer. You have $250,000 in savings and a credit score north of 700. Here's the truth that nobody tells first-time hotel buyers: your local bank will almost certainly say no. This chapter explains why—and shows you the path that actually works.

You call your bank—the one where you've had accounts for fifteen years. The branch manager takes your information, says it sounds interesting, and promises to "run it up the chain." A week passes. You call back. Voicemail. You send an email. No response. On day twelve, you finally reach someone who tells you they "don't do those types of loans."

You try two more banks. One asks for documents, then goes silent. The other says they'd need 35% down—$630,000 in cash you don't have.

Three weeks gone. Your purchase contract has a financing contingency that expires in 45 days. And you're starting to wonder if this deal is even possible.

Here's what's happening: conventional lenders see a business that lives or dies on occupancy rates, seasonal swings, and online reviews. They see a property that requires constant reinvestment—new mattresses, HVAC repairs, parking lot resealing. They see operational risk that an apartment building or strip mall doesn't carry. So they move on to easier deals. This is the Hotelier's Dilemma. To you, that motel represents $200,000 in annual cash flow and a path to financial independence. To a conventional lender, it's a 42-room liability they don't want on their books.

The SBA exists to bridge that gap.

## II. The Core Benefits for Hospitality

Before we examine the specific rules, you must understand why the vast majority of independent hotel acquisitions and small franchise purchases in the United States use SBA financing. It comes down to three specific advantages: Capital Preservation, Cash Flow Management, and Project Versatility.

### Capital Preservation: The Liquidity Lifeline

In the hotel business, cash is oxygen. You will face seasonality where occupancy drops to 40% in January. You will face unexpected Property Improvement Plans (PIPs) from franchisors. You will have boilers break and roofs leak.

If you sink 35% of your cash into the down payment of the building, you leave yourself vulnerable to these operational shocks.

**Conventional Scenario:**

- Purchase Price: $2,000,000
- Down Payment (35%): $700,000
- Closing Costs: $50,000
- Total Cash to Close: $750,000

**SBA 7(a) Scenario:**

- Purchase Price: $2,000,000
- Down Payment (10%): $200,000
- Closing Costs & Guarantee Fee: $100,000 (approximate)
- Total Cash to Close: $300,000

In this comparison, the SBA route leaves you with $450,000 of more liquidity. That is a war chest for marketing, renovations, or surviving a market downturn. For many hoteliers, this difference is not convenient; it is the difference between buying the property and staying on the sidelines.

Consider the return on investment (ROI). If both scenarios generate $200,000 in annual net profit, your cash-on-cash return in the conventional deal is 26%. In the SBA scenario, because your invested cash is lower, your cash-on-cash return jumps to nearly 66%. This use allows you to grow your portfolio faster.

## Cash Flow Management: The Power of 25 Years

Real estate loans under the SBA 7(a) and 504 programs generally offer a 25-year fully amortized term. This is distinct from conventional loans which often amortize over 20 years but balloon (come due in full) in 5 or 10 years.

The monthly difference is substantial. Let us look at the debt service on a $1.5 million loan balance at a hypothetical 8.5% interest rate:

- 20-Year Amortization (Conventional): $13,017 monthly principal and interest.
- 25-Year Amortization (SBA): $12,078 monthly principal and interest.

That saves $1,000 a month. While that may seem small, over the course of a year, that is $12,000. That is enough to pay a part-time housekeeper or cover a significant utility spike. And because there is no balloon payment, you are not at the mercy of interest rates or property values five years from now. You have locked in your financing for a quarter-century.

### Versatility: Bundling the Project

A hotel transaction is rarely a real estate buy.

It involves:

- Land and Building: The physical motel.
- FF&E: Furniture, Fixtures, and Equipment (beds, TVs, ice machines, shuttle vans).
- Goodwill: The business value (reputation, customer lists, future bookings).
- PIP: Renovation costs required by the franchise.
- Inventory: Linens, soap, breakfast supplies.

Conventional lenders often struggle to finance the "Goodwill" or "Blue Sky" portion of the deal. They might lend 75% on the building but zero on the business value. This forces you to come up with even more cash to cover the gap.

The SBA 7(a) program allows you to bundle *all* of these components into a single loan. You do not need a separate equipment loan for the beds and a separate mortgage for the building. It is one closing, one monthly payment, and one set of rules.

## III. The Rules of Engagement: Eligibility

Before you spend hours gathering tax returns, you must ensure you and your target property are eligible. The SBA has specific tripwires for the hospitality industry.

### Citizenship and Ownership Structure

This is a frequent point of confusion. Under current SBA regulations (Policy Notice 5000-876441, effective March 1, 2026), the business must be owned 100% by U.S. Citizens or U.S. Nationals who have their Principal Residence in the United States, its territories, or possessions. Note: Lawful Permanent Residents (Green Card holders) are no longer eligible to own any percentage of an SBA-financed business under this updated rule.

Important Update (March 1, 2026): The previous 5% exception for foreign national ownership has been eliminated. There are no exceptions-100% of ownership must be held by U.S. Citizens or U.S. Nationals residing in the United States.

**The Trap:**

In the past, some percentage of foreign ownership was allowed. This is no longer permitted. As of March 1, 2026 (PN 5000-876441), 100% of ownership must be held by U.S. Citizens or U.S. Nationals. If you have a business partner on an E-2 Investor Visa or H-1B Visa who wants to own 20% of the hotel, this deal is ineligible for SBA financing. Every owner with 20% or more equity must provide a personal guarantee, and every guarantor generally must be a U.S. Citizen or LPR.

### The Passive Activity Rule (Management Agreements)

The SBA requires the borrower to be "active." They do not finance passive real estate investments.

**The Trap:**

You buy a hotel and lease it to an operator who runs it, pays you rent, and keeps the profits. This is ineligible.

**The Fix:**

You must operate the hotel. You can hire a General Manager, but you (the owner) must retain control. You can also hire a professional third-party management company (such as a national management company or a local operator), but the management agreement must strictly preserve your authority.

According to SOP 50 10 8, for a hotel to remain eligible while using a management company, the agreement must give you (the borrower) the following rights:

- Budget Approval: You must approve the annual operating budget.
- Capital Expenditures: You must approve capital expenditures and operating expenses over a significant dollar threshold.
- Bank Accounts: You must have control over the business bank accounts. The management company cannot have sole, unchecked access to the funds.
- Employees: You must have oversight over the employees operating the business.

If the management agreement gives the operator "sole discretion" over these items, the SBA views you as a passive investor, and the loan will be denied.

### Length of Stay (The Apartment Test)

SBA loans are for "transient" lodging.

- The Rule: More than 50% of the revenue must come from guests staying 30 days or less.
- The Danger Zone: Extended Stay motels or "Weekly" rentals. If your property operates more like an apartment building where residents stay for months or years, it may be classified as passive rental income.

Due Diligence Warning: For properties with extended-stay operations, verify that all revenue is properly reported. Some sellers exclude revenue from guests staying more than 30 days from standard reports. SBA eligibility requires more than 50% of revenue from transients staying 30 days or less.

- Pro Tip: If you are buying an Extended Stay franchise (like Residence Inn or Homewood Suites), you are usually safe because the business model is transient by nature. If you are buying a gritty roadside motel with "Weekly Rates" painted on the window, the lender will check the "Rent Roll" or "Guest Ledger" to see how long people stay.

### Character and Legal History

The SBA Form 1920 and Form 1919 require disclosures about criminal history. If you or any 20% owner are currently incarcerated, on parole, or on probation, the loan is ineligible. Past felonies do not automatically disqualify you, but they trigger a "Character Determination" review which can add weeks or months to the process. You must disclose everything; a background check will reveal what you hide, and hiding it is immediate grounds for denial.

## IV. Case Study A: The First-Time Buyer (Raj)

To understand how these rules work in practice, we will follow Raj. Raj has worked as a General Manager for a large hotel group for five years. He knows operations, he knows revenue management, and he is ready to purchase his own asset.

**The Scenario:**

Raj identifies a 40-room independent motel located off a busy highway exit. The property is older but well-maintained. It is not flagged (no franchise like Holiday Inn or Motel 6), which means no royalties, but also no central reservation system.

- Purchase Price: $1.8 million.
- Raj's Cash: He has saved $220,000.
- The Goal: Acquire the business and the real estate.

### The Equity Injection Rule (The 10% Floor)

Under the current regulations (SOP 50 10 8), the SBA requires a minimum equity injection of **10%** of the *Total Project Cost* for a complete change of ownership.

However, many lenders require 15% to 20% in practice. Why

the gap? Closing costs and SBA guarantee fees do not count toward your equity injection. If you bring exactly 10% of the purchase price, you may still come up short after paying appraisal fees, legal costs, title insurance, and the SBA guarantee fee (which can exceed 3% of the loan amount on larger deals). Experienced borrowers plan for 15% to 20% cash to close, even though the SOP only requires 10%.

For Raj, the project cost looks like this:

- Purchase Price: $1,800,000
- Closing Costs & Fees: $55,000
- Working Capital: $50,000 (money to operate the first few months)
- Total Project Cost: $1,905,000

**Required Equity (10%):** $190,500.
Raj has $220,000 saved. This works. He puts in $190,500 and retains $29,500 in personal reserves.

**Reality Check: The "All-In" Danger**
Lenders will look at Raj's "post-closing liquidity." If Raj puts every penny he owns into the deal, the lender may decline the loan even if he meets the 10% rule. Lenders want to see that Raj can pay his personal mortgage and buy groceries if the hotel has a bad first month.

- *Pro Tip:* Raj should try to keep at least 3 to 6 months of personal living expenses separate from his injection funds.

## Acceptable Sources of Equity

Where can Raj get this money? The SBA is strict about "borrowed funds." You cannot simply borrow the down payment from a credit card or an unsecured personal loan, as that adds too much debt to your personal balance sheet.

However, Raj has options:

- Cash: Savings, checking, money market accounts. (Must provide 2 months of bank statements to prove the funds are his and didn't appear yesterday).
- HELOC: A Home Equity Line of Credit on his primary residence.
- *The Rule:* He can use HELOC funds *if* he can show independent repayment ability. This means his other income (a spouse's salary) must be enough to pay the HELOC monthly payment. The hotel's cash flow cannot be relied upon to pay the HELOC.
- Gift Funds: Raj's parents can gift him money.

The Rule: They must sign a "Gift Letter" stating specifically that this is a gift and *not* a loan. There can be no expectation of repayment, ever. A true gift is permanent; the donor is giving money with no strings attached. This is different from a seller standby note (discussed below), which is a loan that remains unpaid during the SBA loan term but may eventually be repaid.

### The Seller Note Strategy

Raj negotiates with the seller. The seller wants $1.8 million but is willing to help Raj get the deal done.

SBA rules allow for **Seller Financing** to count toward the equity injection under specific conditions.

- The Rule: The seller can carry a note on "Full Standby." This means Raj makes *no* payments (principal or interest) to the seller for the life of the SBA loan (usually 25 years) or until the SBA loan is paid off.
- The Limit: Seller debt on full standby can count for *up to half* of the required equity.

**Raj's Revised Deal Structure:**

- Total Project Cost: $1,905,000
- Required Equity (10%): $190,500

- Raj's Cash (5%): $95,250
- Seller Note (5%): $95,250 (on full standby)
- SBA Loan (90%): $1,714,500

By convincing the seller to hold a note for $95,250 on standby, Raj only needs to bring $95,250 of his own cash to the table. This preserves his liquidity significantly.

**Why would a seller agree to "Full Standby"?**

It sounds unappealing to wait 25 years for payment. However, most SBA loans are refinanced or paid off in 5 to 7 years. Once Raj refinances the SBA loan with a conventional bank later, the seller gets paid. The seller agrees to this because it allows them to sell the property *now* to a buyer who otherwise couldn't afford it.

## V. Case Study B: The Renovation & Flag Conversion (Anil)

Now we look at a more complex scenario. Anil is an experienced hotelier. He owns two properties already. He has found a 55-room unbranded motel that has been neglected.

**The Scenario:**

- Purchase Price: $1.9 million.
- The Plan: Convert it to a Choice Hotels franchise (e.g., Comfort Inn or Quality Inn).
- The PIP: The franchisor (Choice) issues a Property Improvement Plan (PIP) requiring $600,000 in renovations (new signage, lobby upgrade, new furniture, bathroom remodels).
- Total Project Need: $2.5 million.

### Dealing with the PIP

In conventional lending, Anil might have to pay for the $600,000 renovation out of pocket or get a high-interest construction bridge loan. The SBA 7(a) program shines here because it allows **PIP financing** to be rolled into the primary acquisition loan.

### The "As Completed" Appraisal

This is the critical mechanic for Anil. The lender will order an appraisal that asks two questions:

- What is the hotel worth *today*? (As Is)
- What will the hotel be worth *after* the $600,000 renovation and the new Franchise Flag is flying? (As Completed)

Usually, the "As Completed" value is higher than the sum of the purchase price plus the renovation costs because a flagged hotel drives higher revenue (RevPAR) than a rundown independent motel.

If the appraiser says the "As Completed" value is $3.2 million, the bank is comfortable lending $2.5 million because the Loan-to-Value (LTV) ratio is healthy (around 78%).

### Managing the Construction Funds

The SBA lender will not hand Anil a check for $600,000 at closing. That money is placed into a **Construction Escrow** account.

- Closing: The $1.9 million is paid to the seller. The $600,000 is held by the bank.
- Draws: As Anil's contractor completes the lobby, they submit an invoice. The bank inspects the work (or gets photos/certification) and releases the funds to pay the contractor.
- Interest Only: During the renovation period (typically 6 to 12 months), Anil only pays interest on the funds that have been disbursed. He does not pay full principal and interest until the project is complete and the hotel is fully operational. This protects his cash flow while rooms are offline for renovation.

## VI. The Environmental Hurdle

There is a step in the hotel loan process that often blindsides buyers: the Environmental Investigation. Hotels are commercially intensive properties. They often house swimming pool chemicals, older hotels may have asbestos, and some are built on corners that used to be gas stations.

Because the SBA acts as an insurer, they want to avoid inheriting a property contaminated by hazardous materials.

### The NAICS Code Trigger

According to SBA SOP 50 10 8, lenders must check the "North American Industry Classification System" (NAICS) codes for the property's *current and past* uses.

Important: While NAICS codes can flag industries with potential environmental concerns, they do not reveal actual previous property use. Only a professional environmental assessment can confirm what activities before occurred on the site.

- Gas Stations: If the hotel was ever a gas station, a Phase I Environmental Site Assessment (ESA) is mandatory.
- Dry Cleaning: If the hotel had on-site dry cleaning (common in older full-service hotels), a Phase I is mandatory.

### The RSRA (Records Search with Risk Assessment)

For most standard hotels that do not have a history of gas or dry cleaning, the lender will start with a Records Search with Risk Assessment. This is a "light" version of an environmental audit. A database company checks government records to see if any nearby properties (like the Jiffy Lube next door) have reported leaks that might migrate to your land.

In practice, many hotels trigger a full Phase I ESA regardless of the RSRA results. Hotels have inherent environmental risk factors:

swimming pools (chemical storage), on-site laundry facilities (solvents and drainage), backup generators (diesel fuel tanks), and often decades of ownership history. An older property built on former agricultural or industrial land may have unknown contamination. Many experienced lenders skip directly to Phase I for hotels because the cost ($1,500 to $3,500) is modest compared to the risk of discovering problems later.

Tip: If contamination was before discovered, obtaining a 'No Further Action' (NFA) letter from the appropriate governmental entity can allow the loan to proceed. This letter confirms no further remediation or monitoring is required.

- Low Risk: If the RSRA comes back "Low Risk," you are done.
- Elevated Risk: If the RSRA shows a risk, the lender must upgrade to a full Phase I ESA.

## Phase I and Phase II

A Phase I ESA involves an environmental engineer walking the property and reviewing historical records. If they find a "Recognized Environmental Condition" (REC)—for example, an old underground heating oil tank that might be leaking—they will recommend a Phase II.

- Phase II: This involves drilling into the soil and testing groundwater. It is expensive ($5,000 - $15,000) and slow.
- The Deal Killer: If the Phase II finds contamination, the seller must remediate it, or you must get an indemnification agreement. Most small business buyers walk away at this point.

**Pro Tip for Anil:** Since Anil is renovating, he should do his own environmental due diligence early. Finding an old oil tank in the middle of a PIP renovation is a financial disaster.

## VII. Refinancing Existing Hotel Debt

SBA loans are not for buying hotels; they are excellent tools for rescuing them from bad debt. Many hoteliers are currently sitting on "bridge loans" or "hard money" loans with interest rates of 10%, 12%, or higher, with balloon payments looming.

You can use an SBA 7(a) loan to refinance this debt, but there are three specific rules you must meet:

### The "10% Improvement" Rule

The SBA requires that the new installment payment amount be at least 10 percent less than the existing installment amount(s).

- *Example:* If your current hard money loan requires interest-only payments of $15,000/month, your new SBA loan payment must be $13,500 or less.
- *Exceptions:* If your current loan has a balloon payment coming due, this rule is automatically satisfied because a balloon payment is considered an "unreasonable financial burden."

### The "Same Institution Debt" (SID) Trap

If you have a loan with Bank A, and you want to refinance it into an SBA loan with Bank A, the SBA gets suspicious. They worry Bank A is trying to take a risky conventional loan and slap an SBA guarantee on it to protect themselves.

> *The Rule:* If a lender refinances their own debt (SID), they cannot use their delegated (fast) authority. The file must go to the SBA Loan Guaranty Processing Center for a full manual review. This adds time and scrutiny.

### The "Current" Rule

You cannot use an SBA loan to bail out a loan that is already in default. You must have been "current" on your existing loan payments for the last 12 months (no payments more than 29 days late). If you are already 60 days late on your mortgage, you generally cannot refinance with the SBA.

## VIII. The Franchise Factor

If you are buying a flagged hotel (Marriott, Hilton, Wyndham, Choice, IHG), the Franchisor is the third party in your marriage with the bank.

### The Franchise Directory

Historical Context: The SBA Franchise Directory replaced the former Franchise Directory. Unlike the Registry, which involved SBA legal review of franchise agreements and FDDs, the Directory primarily functions as a compliance listing. Lenders must still independently verify that agreement terms comply with SBA requirements.

The SBA maintains a "Franchise Directory." Before a lender can approve your loan, they must check if your specific brand is on this list.

- *Good News:* Almost every major hotel brand is on the list.
- *Bad News:* If you are buying a small, obscure franchise, check the directory first. If they aren't listed, the Franchisor must submit their documents to the SBA for review, which takes time.

### The Comfort Letter

This is a critical document. It is a tripartite agreement between the Lender, the Franchisor, and You.

- What it says: It grants the lender the right to step in and operate the hotel under the brand if you foreclose. Without this, a bank would foreclose on a "Marriott" only

to have Marriott strip the flag the next day, destroying the asset's value.
- The Timing: Franchisors are notoriously slow at signing Comfort Letters. Start this process as soon as your loan is approved. Do not wait until the week of closing.

### The PIP Timeline

Ensure your loan term matches your PIP timeline. If the franchise agreement gives you 12 months to finish renovations, but your contractor says it will take 14 months, you have a problem. The SBA lender will require the PIP to be finished to close out the construction escrow. You must align the Franchisor's deadlines with the Lender's disbursement period.

PIP costs are often larger than buyers expect. For mid-scale franchise hotels, expect $10,000 to $40,000 per room. A 60-room property converting to a national flag might face a PIP of $750,000 to $2.4 million. Full-service properties can exceed $4 million. Lenders scrutinize extended PIP timelines because the property serves as collateral while renovations are in progress. A two-year PIP creates more risk than a six-month refresh. If your PIP timeline extends beyond 12 months, expect more documentation requirements and possibly a higher equity contribution.

## IX. Valuations and "Going Concern"

One of the most confusing aspects of hotel financing is the valuation. When you purchase a house, the appraisal is simple: it's worth what the neighbors' houses sold for.

When you purchase a hotel, the appraiser is valuing a "Going Concern." They are allocating value to three distinct buckets. Lenders care deeply about this allocation because it affects collateral.

### Real Property (The Dirt and Bricks)

This is the value of the land and the building itself. If the hotel closed tomorrow, what is the property worth?

*Lender View:* This is the best collateral. It doesn't move or depreciate as fast as furniture.

### Personal Property (FF&E)

This includes the beds, televisions, lobby furniture, shuttle vans, and kitchen equipment.

*Lender View:* This collateral depreciates rapidly. A used hotel mattress has zero resale value.

### Intangible Personal Property (Goodwill/Business Value)

This is the value of the flag (Marriott vs. Joe's Motel), the customer database, the reputation, and the future cash flow exceeding the tangible assets.

- *Lender View:* This is "air" collateral. If the business fails, this value evaporates instantly.

**Why This Matters to You:**

If the appraisal comes back with a heavy allocation to "Intangible Value" (Goodwill), the lender might get nervous. The SBA 7(a) program allows financing of goodwill, but the lender must feel confident that the management team (you) can maintain that value.

Note: Hotel appraisals using the "going concern" method may or may not include goodwill as a separate line item. The income approach values the property based on its earnings potential, which inherently captures business value. Whether that business value is called "goodwill" or simply reflected in the capitalized income figure depends on the appraiser's method. Ask your appraiser to explain exactly how they allocated value between real property, FF&E,

and intangibles. This matters for both lender underwriting and tax purposes.

**The "Business Valuation" Requirement**

If the transaction is a "Change of Ownership" and the amount financed minus the appraised value of real estate and equipment is greater than $250,000, the SBA requires a specific **Business Valuation** from a qualified source (like a Certified Valuation Analyst), separate from the Real Estate Appraisal.

*Anil's Case:* Since he is buying an unbranded motel and renovating it, most of the value is in the real estate potential.

*Raj's Case:* If Raj pays $1.8 million, but the building is only worth $1 million and the FF&E is worth $200k, there is $600k of "Goodwill." The lender will scrutinize why that goodwill exists. Is it because the current owner is amazing? Will it disappear when Raj takes over?

## X. Comparing the Programs: 7(a) vs. 504 for Hotels

So far, we have focused mainly on the 7(a) program, which is the most common for hotel acquisitions under $5 million. However, the SBA 504 program is a powerful alternative, especially for larger projects.

You must choose the right tool for the job.

### SBA 7(a): The Swiss Army Knife

- Structure: One loan from one bank. The SBA guarantees a portion of it.
- Maximum Loan: The *total* loan amount is capped at $5 million (this is the loan amount, not the guaranteed portion).

- Interest Rate: Typically variable (Prime Rate + a margin, e.g., Prime + 2%). Some lenders offer fixed rates, but variable is standard.
- Uses: Can buy the building, the business, the equipment, and provide working capital.
- Down Payment: Minimum 10%.
- Prepayment Penalty: Only for the first 3 years (5% year 1, 3% year 2, 1% year 3).
- Best For: Raj and Anil. Projects under $5 million where simplicity and lower down payments are priorities.

## SBA 504: The Heavy Lifter

Structure: Three parts.

1. Bank Loan (50%): A conventional mortgage from a bank.
2. CDC Debenture (30-35%): A loan from a Certified Development Company (CDC) backed by the SBA.
3. Borrower Equity (15-20%): Your cash.

    - Maximum SBA Contribution: The CDC portion is capped at $5 million (or $5.5 million for green projects). However, because the bank portion is unlimited, the *total* project size can be $15 million, $20 million, or more.

    - Interest Rate: The CDC portion is fixed for 20 or 25 years at a low market rate. The bank portion is negotiated (often fixed for 5-10 years).

    - The "Special Purpose" Catch: The SBA classifies hotels as "Special Purpose Properties." Under the 504 rules, this triggers a penalty on use.

    * Standard 504 equity is 10%.

    * Hotel 504 equity is 15%.

- * If you are a New Business (start-up) buying a hotel, equity is 20%.
- Uses: Strictly for fixed assets (Real Estate and heavy equipment). Cannot be used for working capital, inventory, or goodwill.
- Prepayment Penalty: The CDC portion has a 10-year declining prepayment penalty.
- Best For: Large projects (over $5 million) where locking in a fixed interest rate is more important than a low down payment.

### The Decision Matrix

- Choose 7(a) If: You need to finance Goodwill/Business value, you want the lowest possible down payment (10%), or you plan to sell or refinance within 5 years (short prepayment penalty).
- Choose 504 If: Your project is massive ($8M+), you plan to hold the property for 20 years, and you want a fixed interest rate to protect against inflation.

## XI. The Costs: Fees and Guarantees

SBA financing is not free money. It comes with specific costs that you must budget for.

### The SBA Guaranty Fee

The SBA charges a fee for providing the insurance policy to the bank. This fee is usually passed on to you, the borrower.

- The fee is based on the *guaranteed portion* of the loan, not the total loan.
- For loans over $1 million, the fee is substantial. It is 3.5% to 3.75% of the guaranteed portion.

- *Example:* On a $2 million loan (75% guaranteed), the fee could be around $50,000 to $60,000.
- *Good News:* You can roll this fee into the loan amount. You do not need to pay it in cash.

### The Personal Guarantee

This is often the hardest pill for investors to swallow.

- The Rule: Any person who owns 20% or more of the borrowing entity must personally guarantee the loan.
- No Exceptions: You cannot hide behind an LLC. If the hotel fails and the foreclosure sale doesn't cover the loan balance, the bank and the SBA can come after your personal assets (house, savings, other investments).
- Spouses: If you own 100% of the business, but you have few personal assets and your spouse has a high-paying job or assets, the lender *might* require the spouse to guarantee as well.

## XII. Potential Pitfalls and How to Avoid Them

Even with a perfect property, hotel deals die in underwriting every day. Here are the common mistakes:

### The Resume Gap

The lender is betting on *you* to fill the rooms.

- Mistake: "I'm an IT professional, I've never run a hotel, but I travel a lot."
- Fix: If you lack direct experience, you must partner with someone who has it, or hire a reputable third-party management company. The lender needs to see a "Hotelier's Resume" in the file.

### Projections that Defy Gravity

- Mistake: The hotel historically runs at 50% occupancy. You submit a business plan claiming you will hit 85% in Year 1 because you are "better."
- Fix: Be conservative. If you project revenue growth, you must justify it with specific data (e.g., "A new convention center is opening next door" or "We are adding 10 rooms"). You must justify why you can beat the market trends.

### Ignoring the PIP

- Mistake: Underestimating the cost of the franchise renovation.
- Fix: Get a formal PIP estimate from the franchisor or a contractor before you finalize your loan application. If you borrow $300k for a PIP that costs $500k, you will run out of money halfway through, and the hotel will not open.

## XIII. Decision Matrix: Is SBA Right for You?

Use this summary to make your final determination before moving to the next chapter.

**Choose SBA 7(a) If:**

- Liquidity is Priority: You want to put only 10-15% down.
- Project Size: The total deal is under $5 million.
- Scope: You are buying a business, doing a renovation (PIP), and need working capital all in one loan.
- Timeline: You plan to refinance or sell the hotel in 5-7 years (lower prepayment penalty).
- Structure: You are buying an independent boutique hotel or a franchise.

**Consider Conventional Financing If:**

- Cash is Abundant: You have 35-40% down and want to avoid the SBA Guaranty Fee.
- Collateral Rich: You have other unencumbered real estate to pledge.
- Speed: You need to close in 30 days (SBA typically takes 45-90 days).
- Privacy: You refuse to sign a personal guarantee (though many conventional banks require this too).

**Choose SBA 504 If:**

- Project Size: The deal is over $5 million.
- Rate Sensitive: You absolutely demand a long-term fixed interest rate on a portion of the debt.
- Capital: You can afford a 15-20% down payment (due to the Special Purpose rule).

## XIV. Next Steps

If you have decided that SBA financing fits your hotel acquisition strategy, your immediate next steps are:

- Prepare your "Hotelier's Resume": Detail your management experience or identify your management partner.
- Sourcing Your Cash: Gather 2 months of bank statements to prove where your injection is coming from. If it's a gift, get the letter ready.
- Organize Financials: You need SBA Form 413 (Personal Financial Statement), 3 years of tax returns (personal and business), and an Interim Balance Sheet dated within the last 120 days.
- Engage the Franchisor (if applicable): Start the application for the franchise flag and request the PIP.

- Find a Specialist Lender: Do not walk into any bank. You need a lender who understands Hospitality *and* SBA. They are distinct skill sets.

In the following chapters, we will break down exactly how to prepare these documents and how to negotiate the best terms for your hotel loan.

CHAPTER 2

# DO YOU QUALIFY? ELIGIBILITY REQUIREMENTS FOR HOTELS

What if you could know, before spending weeks gathering documents, whether your hotel deal qualifies for SBA financing? Here's the secret that experienced hotel buyers understand: eligibility isn't about your credit score or how much money you have. It's about rules that most people never hear about until their deal is dead. This chapter gives you that answer in fifteen minutes.

You have found a property. The numbers look reasonable. The location shows promise. You are ready to move forward. But before you spend a single dollar on appraisals, environmental reports, or franchise application fees, you must answer one fundamental question: Is this deal eligible for an SBA loan?

You might assume that because they are a small business, they are automatically eligible. This is a dangerous assumption. The SBA has a specific, rigid set of rules governing who gets in and who stays out. For hotel and motel owners, these rules are even more specific. There are requirements about how long your guests stay, who manages the front desk, how your legal entities are structured, and even what brand name hangs on the sign outside.

Eligibility is binary. You are either eligible, or you are not. There is little gray area in the Standard Operating Procedures (SOP) used by lenders. If you violate a core eligibility rule, no amount of collateral or high credit scores will save the deal. The loan will be denied.

In this chapter, we will walk through the eligibility requirements in detail. We will look at the specific hurdles that hoteliers face, using the same two borrowers we introduced in Chapter 1.

**Recall that Raj is acquiring a 40-room independent highway motel for $1.8 million with $220,000 in savings. Anil, our experienced operator, is pursuing a $2.5 million project to acquire and convert a 55-room motel to a Choice Hotels flag.**

Both face potential eligibility traps that could kill their deals if they are not careful. Let us examine exactly what the lender requires.

## I. The Core Eligibility Test: Active vs. Passive Operations

The Small Business Administration was created to help active small businesses. It was not created to help passive real estate investors. This distinction is the single most important concept in hotel lending.

If you purchase an office building and rent it out to a law firm, you are a landlord. That is a passive activity. You collect a check, fix the roof occasionally, and pay the taxes. That is not eligible for a standard SBA 7(a) loan.

Hotels sit in a conceptual middle ground. You are technically renting rooms, which sounds like being a landlord. However, you are also providing maid service, front desk concierge, breakfast, and security. That sounds like an active business. To clear up this confusion, the SBA has established a bright-line rule about the nature of your guests.

### The "Transient" Requirement

To be eligible for SBA financing, a hotel, motel, or similar lodging facility must derive more than 50% of its revenue from transients who stay for 30 days or less at a time.

This is often called the "Transient Rule." The SBA wants to ensure you are running a hospitality business, not an apartment complex or a long-term housing facility.

**Why This Matters**

If you are buying a standard hotel near an airport, this rule is easy to meet. Your guests stay for one or two nights. However, if you are buying a motel in a rural area or a city with a housing shortage, you might find that the current owner has filled the rooms with long-term residents.

If 60% of the revenue comes from locals paying a weekly rate who have lived there for six months, the property is ineligible. It is considered an apartment complex in the eyes of the SBA.

**Application to Raj (The Independent Motel)**

Raj is looking at a highway motel. It is unbranded, meaning it is "Raj's Highway Inn." Because it does not have a national reservation system feeding it nightly guests, Raj needs to look closely at the "Rent Roll" or the "Daily Flash Reports" from the seller.

**The Risk:** If the previous owner decided to rent 25 of the 40 rooms to local construction crews who signed six-month contracts, Raj has a problem. If those contracts generate the majority of the income, the deal dies.

The Fix: Raj must verify the guest history. If the long-term stays are high but under 50% of revenue, he is safe. If they are over 50%, he faces a difficult situation. He cannot simply promise to change it. Lenders look at historical tax returns. If the tax returns show "Rental Income" on Schedule E than "Lodging Income" or "Gross Receipts" on Schedule C (or Form 1065/1120), it triggers a red flag.

**Start-Up Exception:** If Raj were building a new motel from the ground up, he would not have a history. In that specific case, the SBA allows eligibility based on *projections*. Raj would need to submit a business plan and a feasibility study showing that the business model targets nightly travelers and that he expects >50% of revenue from short-term guests.

**Application to Anil (The Flagged Hotel)**

Anil is converting his property to a Choice Hotels brand. Most major hotel brands (Marriott, Hilton, IHG, Choice, Wyndham) have strict rules prohibiting long-term residency because it damages brand standards.

**The Result:** Because Anil is adopting a flag, the lender will generally assume the business model meets the transient requirement. The nature of a franchised hotel implies nightly stays. Anil still needs to certify this, but he will face less scrutiny than Raj.

## The Passive Business Trap: Management Agreements

The second part of the "Active vs. Passive" test involves how the hotel is run. The SBA requires the borrower (you) to be actively involved. You cannot simply buy the hotel and hand the keys to a third-party management company that runs everything without your input.

This does not mean you have to clean the rooms or stand behind the front desk. You are allowed to hire a management company. However, the contract between you and that management company is subject to intense scrutiny.

**The Rule of "Sole Discretion"**

The SBA rule states that a business is ineligible if it enters into a management agreement that gives the management company "sole discretion" over the business operations.

If the management company can hire and fire staff, set the

budget, sign checks, and make capital improvements without asking you, the SBA views you as a passive investor. You are providing the money while someone else runs the business. That makes you ineligible.

**Required "Meaningful Oversight"**

To remain eligible while using a management company, you must retain "Meaningful Oversight." Your management agreement must explicitly state that you (the owner/borrower) retain the final say on specific items.

**The Checklist for Management Agreements:**

To pass SBA review, the agreement must reserve the following rights for the owner:

- Budget Approval: The owner must approve the annual operating budget.
- Capital Expenditures: The owner must approve capital expenditures (repairs/upgrades) and operating expenses over a specific dollar threshold.
- Bank Accounts: The owner must have control over the business bank accounts. The management company can be a signer, but the owner must be the primary controller.
- Employees: The people working at the hotel must be employees of the Applicant (the owner's company), not the management company. The management company can supervise them, but the owner signs the paychecks.

**Reality Check:** Many standard hotel management contracts used by large firms are written to give the manager total control. These standard contracts will result in an automatic decline from the SBA. You must add an addendum or rewrite the contract to meet SBA standards.

**Application to Anil**
Anil owns three properties now. He cannot be in three places at once. He decides to hire "Premier Hotel Management LLC" to run the new Choice Hotel.

**The Risk:** Premier sends Anil their standard contract. Clause 4 says: *"Manager shall have the exclusive right to hire, fire, and supervise all personnel."* Clause 6 says: *"Manager shall have sole authority over all operating accounts."*

**The Fix:** If Anil signs this, his loan is denied. Anil must work with his SBA lender to draft an "SBA Addendum" to the management agreement. This addendum will state: *"Notwithstanding any other provision, the Owner retains final authority over the budget, bank accounts, and employment decisions."*

**Pro Tip:** Do not sign a management agreement before showing it to your lender. Send the draft to your banker first. They will send it to their closing department to "redline" (edit) it for compliance. This saves weeks of legal headaches later.

## II. Size Standards: Are You Small Enough?

The SBA is the *Small* Business Administration. They cannot lend to giant corporations. However, "small" in the hotel industry is large compared to other sectors.

You must qualify as a small business under one of two standards: the Industry Standard (Receipts) or the Alternative Standard (Net Worth/Income).

### The Industry Size Standard (The $40 Million Cap)

The SBA uses NAICS codes (North American Industry Classification System) to define industries. Most hotels fall under NAICS 721110 (Hotels and Motels) or 721120 (Casino Hotels).

Under current regulations (13 CFR 121.201), the size standard for hotels is based on **average annual receipts**.

- The Cap: $40.0 Million.
- The Calculation: This is the average annual receipts of the business (and its affiliates) over the last three to five years.

If you own or are affiliated with other hotels, verify your combined revenues do not exceed the $40 million threshold. Different hospitality subcategories have different thresholds: Bed-and-Breakfast Inns (NAICS 721191) and All Other Traveler Accommodation (NAICS 721199) have a $9 million size standard. Check the current SBA size standards table at sba.gov before assuming eligibility.

**Important Definition:** "Receipts" means "Total Income" (gross income) plus "Cost of Goods Sold" (COGS). Many hotel owners forget to add COGS back in. If your hotel has a restaurant or bar, you likely have significant COGS. You must add that number to your Gross Profit to get the correct "Receipts" figure for SBA sizing.

### Application to Raj

Raj is buying a single motel with $600,000 in annual revenue. He has no other businesses.

- Receipts: $600,000.
- Limit: $40,000,000.
- Result: Raj is easily eligible.

### Application to Anil

Anil is more complex. He owns two other hotels and is buying a third.

- Hotel A Receipts: $3.5 Million.
- Hotel B Receipts: $4.2 Million.
- Target Hotel C Projected Receipts: $1.5 Million.
- Total Combined Receipts: $9.2 Million.

**Result:** Anil is well under the $40 million cap. He is still a "small" business.

Reality Check: You might be wondering who hits the $40 million cap. This usually affects owners with 10 to 15 properties. If you own ten Hampton Inns doing $4 million each, you are right at the limit. For most person operators, the revenue cap is not a barrier.

### The Alternative Size Standard

What if you *do* exceed the revenue cap? Anil owns a successful distribution company in addition to his hotels, pushing his group revenue over $40 million. Does he lose eligibility?

Not necessarily. He can try to qualify under the **Alternative Size Standard**.

To qualify here, the business (including affiliates) must meet two tests:

- Tangible Net Worth: Not more than $20 million.
- Average Net Income: Average net income *after* Federal income taxes (excluding carry-over losses) for the preceding two full fiscal years must be not more than $6.5 million.

This is a safety net. Hotels often have high revenue but high expenses (labor, utilities, franchise fees) and significant depreciation. This means a hotel group might have $50 million in revenue but only $3 million in taxable net income. In that case, they would still qualify as small under the Alternative Standard.

## III. Understanding Affiliation

We established that you must combine your affiliates to see if you are small enough. But how does the SBA define an "Affiliate"?

This is an area where many borrowers get confused. The SBA does not look at the specific LLC buying the property. They look at the person behind the deal. If you own other businesses, the SBA considers them "Affiliates."

**The Rule:** To determine size, you must add together the revenue (or net worth/income) of the Applicant business PLUS all Affiliate businesses.

### Affiliation Based on Ownership (The 50% Rule)

This is the most common form of affiliation.

- Clear Control: If you own more than 50% of the Applicant business and more than 50% of another business, those two businesses are affiliates.
- Example: Anil owns 100% of Hotel A. He owns 100% of Hotel B. He will own 100% of the new Target Hotel. Therefore, all three are affiliates.

**Pro Tip:** If you own 50% exactly, and your partner owns 50% exactly, you both have "negative control" (the power to block action). In this case, your other businesses might still be affiliated if your partner also has an interest in them.

### Affiliation Based on Management

Affiliation arises where one or more officers, directors, managing members, or partners who control the management of one concern also control the management of another concern.

**Scenario:** Anil's brother, Sunil, does not own any part of the hotels. However, Sunil is listed as the "Manager" or "President" of Hotel A, Hotel B, and the new Target Hotel in the LLC operating agreements. Because Sunil controls the management of all three, the SBA treats them as affiliates, even though the ownership might be different.

### Totality of the Circumstances

The SBA reserves the right to find affiliation even if no single rule is triggered. If the SBA determines that clear ties of economic dependence or identity of interest exist, they can aggregate the businesses.

**Scenario:** Anil owns Hotel A. His wife owns Hotel B. They operate them as a single unit—sharing staff, sharing a laundry facility, and commingling funds. Even though they file separate taxes and have separate ownership names, the SBA will likely view them as affiliated based on the "Totality of Circumstances."

### Affiliation Through Loan Guarantees

Here is where borrowers get caught: Even if your ownership stake is below 20%, guaranteeing someone else's SBA loan creates contingent liability that affects your application.

Example: Raj owns 15% of his cousin's hotel and signed as a guarantor on the cousin's $1.5 million SBA loan. When Raj applies for his own SBA loan, the lender must factor in his potential liability on the cousin's loan. If the cousin's hotel fails, Raj is on the hook—and so is his ability to repay his own loan.

What Lenders Will Ask:

- Do you own 20% or more of any other business?
- Have you guaranteed any other SBA loans?
- Are there common officers, directors, or key employees between your business and another?

Disclose everything. If the lender discovers undisclosed affiliations or guaranties after approval, the loan can be recalled.

## Why Affiliation Matters for Documents

Understanding affiliation is not about the size cap. It determines the paperwork burden.

**The Requirement:** You must provide tax returns and financial statements for **all** affiliate businesses.

**Application to Anil:**
Anil cannot submit the financials for the hotel he is buying. Because he has two existing hotels (affiliates), the lender must collect the last two to three years of tax returns for Hotel A and Hotel B.

- Why? The lender needs to calculate the Global Cash Flow. They need to ensure Anil's other hotels are not bleeding cash. If Hotel A is losing $500,000 a year, it could drain the cash from the new hotel, causing a default. The lender assesses the health of the entire group.

## IV. Franchises and Flags: The SBA Directory

For decades, franchise eligibility was the hardest part of SBA lending. Lenders had to read 300-page Franchise Disclosure Documents (FDDs) to see if the franchisor exerted "too much control" over the borrower.

That has changed. The SBA now maintains the SBA Franchise Directory—a centralized list of eligible brands (see earlier chapter for details).

### The Directory Rule

The Rule: If your business operates under a franchise, license, or dealer agreement (a "Flag"), that brand must be listed on the SBA Franchise Directory.

It does not matter if the brand is famous. If "Marriott" fell off the list (unlikely), you could not finance a Marriott.

### How to Check

The Directory is a public PDF file hosted on the SBA website. It is updated regularly. It lists:

- The Brand Name.
- The SBA Franchise Identifier Code (e.g., S01234).
- Whether an "Addendum" is required.

**The SBA Addendum (Form 2462):**
Many franchises have clauses in their contracts that the SBA dislikes (e.g., the right to force you to sell the hotel or the right to step in and manage it without your consent). To fix this, the SBA created a standard two-page Addendum. If the Directory says an Addendum is required, the Franchisor *must* sign this document. It overrides the problematic clauses in the franchise agreement.

## Application to Raj (Independent)
Raj is buying "Raj's Highway Inn." There is no franchise agreement. There are no royalty fees.

- Directory Check: Not required.
- Lender Verification: The lender must simply confirm in their credit memo that the business is independent. They may check to ensure Raj isn't signing a "license agreement" or "membership agreement" with a marketing group that acts like a franchise. If he joins "Best Americas Budget Inns" marketing group, that agreement might trigger the Franchise Rule.

## Application to Anil (Choice Hotels)
Anil is converting the motel to a Choice Hotels brand (e.g., Comfort Inn or Quality Inn).

- Step 1: The lender checks the Directory. "Choice Hotels International" is listed.
- Step 2: The lender notes the "SBA Franchise Identifier Code" (e.g., S2267). This code must be entered into the SBA's E-Tran computer system to get the loan number.
- Step 3: The lender checks if an Addendum is required. Most major brands have negotiated a "Global Addendum" with the SBA, meaning they don't need to sign the Form 2462 for every single deal. The Directory will explicitly state if a "2018 Addendum" or similar is on file.

Pro Tip for Anil: If Anil was choosing a small, new, or obscure hotel brand, he should check the Directory *before* signing the franchise agreement. If the brand is not on the list, the franchisor must submit their documents to the SBA for review. This can take weeks. If they refuse to submit, the loan is dead.

## V. Citizenship and Legal Status

The SBA is a U.S. government agency funded by American taxpayers. As such, there are strict rules about who can benefit from these government-guaranteed loans.

### The 100% Rule

SBA financing is limited to businesses where 100% of the direct and indirect owners are U.S. Citizens or U.S. Nationals with Principal Residence in the United States (PN 5000-876441, effective March 1, 2026). Note: Lawful Permanent Residents (Green Card holders) are no longer eligible.

**The Trap:** It is not 51%. It is 100%.
If Anil decides to bring in a "silent partner" to help with the down payment, and that partner is anyone other than a U.S. Citizen or U.S. National residing in the United States, the entire loan is ineligible. Even if the partner only owns 1% of the LLC, the deal cannot proceed under SBA 7(a) rules. This includes Green Card holders, who are no longer eligible as of March 1, 2026.

**Clarification:**

- U.S. Citizens: Eligible.
- Lawful Permanent Residents (Green Card holders): No longer eligible as of March 1, 2026 (PN 5000-876441). Only U.S. Citizens and U.S. Nationals with Principal

Residence in the United States may own any portion of an SBA-financed business.
- Visa Holders (H-1B, E-2, etc.): Generally Ineligible for 7(a) loans as owners. If an owner is here on a work visa, they cannot own any part of the borrowing entity.

**Application to Raj and Anil:**
Both Raj and Anil are U.S. Citizens. They provide copies of their passports or birth certificates. Eligibility cleared.

### Ineligible Persons

Beyond citizenship, the SBA maintains a list of "Ineligible Persons." The business is ineligible if any Associate (officer, director, owner of 20%+) is:
- Incarcerated, on parole, or on probation.
- Currently under indictment for a felony or a crime of moral turpitude.
- An undocumented alien.

## VI. The "Bad Boy" Clauses: Character and History

Finally, we must touch on the "Character" requirements. The SBA will not lend to individuals who they deem to have "poor character." This is determined largely through criminal background checks.

### Form 1919: Statement of Personal History

Every owner with 20% or more equity (and sometimes key managers) must fill out SBA Form 1919. It asks three specific questions about criminal history:
- Are you currently under indictment? (If Yes -> Automatic Decline).
- Have you ever been arrested in the last 6 months?

- Have you ever been convicted, pleaded guilty, pleaded nolo contendere, been placed on pretrial diversion, or been placed on any form of parole or probation (including probation before judgment) for any criminal offense?

**The "Ever" Rule:** Question 3 covers your entire life. If you got a DUI in college 20 years ago, you must check "Yes." If you were arrested 15 years ago and the charges were dropped, you must check "Yes" (because you were arrested/charged).

**Reality Check:** Checking "Yes" does not mean you are denied. It means you must provide a written explanation and court documents showing the case is closed.

- *Raj's Speeding Ticket:* Minor traffic violations (fine <$500) generally do not need to be reported unless they involved drugs or alcohol.
- *Raj's DUI:* If Raj had a DUI 10 years ago, he discloses it. He writes a statement: "I made a mistake in college. I paid my fine and completed my community service. I have not had any issues since." The SBA usually clears this (called a "Background Check clearance").
- *Fingerprints:* If you answer "Yes" to question 3, you will likely need to go to a police station or a LiveScan facility to provide fingerprints. The FBI runs a check. This adds time to the process (2-4 weeks usually).

**The Deal Killers:**

- Crimes of Moral Turpitude: Convictions for fraud, embezzlement, larceny, or financial crimes are often permanent bars to SBA lending. If you have a history of stealing money, the government will not guarantee a loan for you.
- Violent Felonies: Recent violent felonies are also usually disqualifying.

- Open Cases: If you are currently on probation or have an open court case, you are ineligible until the case is fully resolved and probation is finished.

### Prior Loss to the Government

This is a separate check from the criminal history. The lender will run a check in a government database called CAIVRS.

**The Rule:** The SBA will not approve a loan if you have a "Prior Loss" to the government.

- Did you default on a student loan?
- Did you default on an FHA mortgage?
- Did you default on a previous SBA loan?

If the government lost money on you in the past, they generally will not lend to you again. If you have a delinquent federal debt (like unpaid taxes), you must pay it current or have an approved payment plan before you can get an SBA loan.

## VII. Ineligible Business Models for Hotels

Even if you (the person) are eligible, the business itself must be eligible. We already discussed the Passive/Active rule. Here are other business models that disqualify hotels.

### Gambling (The 1/3 Rule)

This is vital for hotels that might have a small casino or video lottery terminals.

**The Rule:** A business is ineligible if it derives more than **one-third** of its annual gross revenue from legal gambling activities.

If Anil buys a hotel in Nevada that has a casino floor, he must prove that the room revenue and food/beverage revenue make up at least 67% of the total income. If the gambling revenue is 40%, the loan is denied.

### Marijuana and Hemp

The SBA is a federal agency. Marijuana is illegal at the federal level.

**The Rule:** Businesses that derive revenue from marijuana-related activities are ineligible.

**Scenario:** Raj buys a motel in Colorado (where marijuana is legal). He wants to lease the retail space in the lobby to a cannabis dispensary.

**Result:** Ineligible. Even leasing space to a marijuana business makes Raj's hotel ineligible because he is receiving "tainted" rent money.

### Speculation

The SBA does not lend for speculation. You cannot buy a hotel, shut it down, hold it for two years hoping the land value goes up, and then sell it. You must operate it as a business.

## VIII. Financial Eligibility: Equity and Project Costs

You qualify as active. You are small enough. Your franchise is approved. Your record is clean. Now, do you have enough money?

SBA loans are high-use (up to 90% loan-to-value), but they are not 100% financing. You must have skin in the game. This is called the Equity Injection.

### Change of Ownership Requirements

For a "Change of Ownership" (buying an existing business), the SBA rules state that the lender must determine if the equity is enough. However, for a *complete* change of ownership, the SBA considers a minimum of 10% equity injection to be necessary for the deal to be sound.

**The Rule:** The equity must be at least 10% of the **Total Project Cost**.

**What is Included in Project Cost?**

- Purchase Price of the Hotel.
- Renovations / PIP (Property Improvement Plan).
- Furniture, Fixtures, and Equipment (FF&E).
- Closing Costs (Legal, SBA Guarantee Fee, Third-party reports).
- Working Capital.

## Start-Up Requirements

If you are building a hotel from scratch (New Construction) or buying a closed hotel to reopen it (which is treated as a start-up), the rules are stricter.

**The Rule:** Start-up businesses **must** inject at least 10% equity. This is non-negotiable and statutory.

## Application to Raj (The Simple Acquisition)

Raj is buying the motel for $1.8 million. He needs some working capital and closing costs, but no major renovations.

- Purchase Price: $1,800,000
- Closing Costs/Fees: $50,000
- Working Capital: $50,000
- Total Project: $1,900,000

**Required Equity:** 10% of $1,900,000 = **$190,000.**

Raj has $220,000 saved. He is eligible.

## Application to Anil (Acquisition + Renovation)

Anil's deal is heavier. He is buying a fixer-upper.

- Purchase Price: $1,700,000
- PIP (Property Improvement Plan) / Renovation: $600,000

- Closing Costs/Fees: $100,000
- Working Capital: $100,000
- Total Project: $2,500,000

**Required Equity:** 10% of $2,500,000 = **$250,000.**

Vital Point: Notice that Anil pays 10% of the renovation cost upfront. He does not pay 10% of the purchase price. The bank is lending on the *future* value of the hotel after renovation, so the equity is calculated on the *total* cost to get there.

## Source of Equity and the 60-Day Rule

Lenders are required to "source and season" your money. You cannot show up to closing with a suitcase of cash. You must provide two months of bank statements showing the money sitting in your account.

If a large deposit appears on the statement, you must explain it. "I sold a car," "I received a tax refund," or "I transferred it from my business account."

**Pro Tip:** Do not move money around between accounts right before applying. It creates a paperwork nightmare of tracing transfers. Keep your down payment funds in one stable account for 60 days before applying.

## The Seller Note: Can It Count as Equity?

This is a common question. Can the seller lend you part of the down payment?

**The Rule:** Seller debt can count toward your equity requirement **ONLY IF** it is on **Full Standby** for the life of the SBA loan.

- "Full Standby" means you make no payments (principal or interest) to the seller for as long as the SBA loan exists (usually 25 years).
- Interest can accrue, but you cannot pay it.

Most sellers will not agree to wait 25 years for their money. Therefore, seller notes are usually *in addition* to your 10% cash, not *instead* of it.

- *Example:* Raj puts in 10% cash. The bank puts in 80%. The Seller carries a note for 10% that Raj pays monthly. This is allowed, but the Seller Note here does not count as Raj's equity. It is another loan.

## IX. The "Credit Elsewhere" Test

SBA loans are a government program designed to help those who cannot get reasonable financing from conventional sources. By law, the SBA cannot lend to you if you can get a regular commercial loan on reasonable terms without the SBA guarantee.

This is known as the **Credit Elsewhere Test**.

### The Liquid Assets Test

The lender must certify that you do not have enough personal liquidity to do the deal yourself.

**Application to Anil:**
Anil is wealthy. He has $5 million in cash sitting in a brokerage account. He wants to borrow $2.5 million for this new hotel.

- The Problem: The SBA might look at Anil and say, "Why should the taxpayers guarantee this loan? You have $5 million liquid. You can write a check for the whole project without hurting your ability to support yourself."
- The Result: Anil might be deemed ineligible because he has "Credit Available Elsewhere" (his own pocket).

**The Exceptions:** The lender can often argue that Anil needs that liquidity to support his other hotels, or for personal family reserves.

However, if your liquid assets exceed the project size, you may face hurdles.

## X. Occupancy and Environmental Rules

Real estate eligibility has physical requirements as well.

### Occupancy Requirements

The SBA requires you to occupy the building. You cannot use an SBA loan to purchase a building and rent it out to others (that's passive).

- Acquisition of Existing Building: You (the hotel operating company) must occupy at least 51% of the rentable property.
- New Construction: You must occupy at least 60% of the rentable property now, growing to other portions later.

**The Hotel Trap (Leasing the Restaurant):**

Hotels are usually 100% owner-occupied. However, some hotels have large restaurant spaces or retail shops attached to the lobby.

- Scenario: Raj's motel has a 4,000 sq. ft. restaurant attached to a 3,000 sq. ft. lobby/office area (the guest rooms count as owner-occupied). Raj decides to lease the restaurant to a local diner chain.
- The Math: If the leased space (restaurant) exceeds 49% of the total square footage, the building becomes ineligible. Raj must be careful about how much space he leases to third parties.

### Environmental Eligibility

Hotels are listed in the SBA SOP as an "Environmentally Sensitive Industry." Why?

- Laundry: Old hotels often had on-site dry cleaning facilities. Dry cleaning solvents (PERC) are hazardous and can contaminate the soil.
- Pools: Improper storage of pool chemicals can be an issue.
- Historical Use: Was the hotel built on an old gas station site?

**The Requirement:** You will almost certainly need a **Phase I Environmental Site Assessment**. An engineer will inspect the property and historical records.

- Clean Phase I: You are good to go.
- Dirty Phase I: If the report finds "Recognized Environmental Conditions" (RECs), you must do a Phase II (soil testing). If contamination is found, the loan is usually dead unless you can remediate it (clean it up) before closing, which is expensive and time-consuming.

## XI. Refinancing Debt

Many hotel owners come to the SBA not to purchase, but to refinance—perhaps you have a high-interest "hard money" loan or a bank loan that is ballooning (coming due).

**The Rule:** To be eligible for SBA refinancing, the new loan must provide a "Substantial Benefit" to the borrower.

- Definition: The new loan payment must be at least 10% lower than the current loan payment.

**Eligible Debt:** You can only refinance debt that was used for eligible business purposes (buying the hotel, renovations). You cannot refinance a personal loan you took to purchase a boat, even if you used the hotel as collateral.

## XII. Structure: EPC / OC (The Hotel Standard)

We alluded to this earlier, but we must formalize it. Most hotels are not owned by a single company. They use a split structure for liability and tax reasons.

- Eligible Passive Company (EPC): This entity (e.g., "Raj Real Estate LLC") owns the land and the building.
- Operating Company (OC): This entity (e.g., "Raj Hotel Operations Inc") leases the building from the EPC and runs the hotel. It hires the staff and collects the guest revenue.

**Why do this?** If a guest slips in the shower and sues the hotel, they sue the Operating Company. The Real Estate entity (which holds the valuable asset) is protected.

**SBA Eligibility for EPC/OC:**

Normally, the EPC (Real Estate holder) would be a passive landlord (ineligible). However, the SBA allows this specific exception **IF**:

- The EPC leases 100% of the property to the OC.
- The lease term matches the loan term (e.g., 25 years).
- The lease payments are enough to cover the loan payments.
- Both the EPC and the OC are co-borrowers or guarantors on the loan.

**Application to Raj:**

Raj should set up two LLCs. "Raj Propco LLC" and "Raj Opco LLC."

- The Lender makes the loan to *both* entities (or Propco as borrower and Opco as guarantor).
- The check buys the building in the name of Propco.
- Opco signs the lease.
- This is fully eligible and highly recommended.

## XIII. Summary Checklist for Hotel Eligibility

Before you submit your application, run your deal through this final checklist. If you can check every box, you are ready for the next step: Creditworthiness.

**The Hotel Eligibility Checklist**

- ☐ Transient Nature: Will >50% of revenue come from guests staying <30 days? (For start-ups, do projections show this?)
- ☐ Active Management: If you have a management company, do you retain approval over the budget, bank accounts, and capital expenditures?
- ☐ Size Standard: Is the combined receipts (Income + COGS) of the hotel and all your affiliates under $40 million? (Or do you meet the Net Worth/Income alternative?)
- ☐ Affiliation: Have you identified all businesses where you have ownership or management control? Are you prepared to submit financials for all of them?
- ☐ Franchise: Is your hotel brand listed on the SBA Franchise Directory?
- ☐ Citizenship: Is the borrowing entity 100% owned by U.S. Citizens or U.S. Nationals with Principal Residence in the U.S.? (Note: Green Card holders no longer eligible as of March 1, 2026)
- ☐ Character: Do you have a clean criminal record (or disclosed and cleared minor offenses)? Are you free of federal debt defaults (Student loans, FHA)?
- ☐ Ineligible Businesses: Is gambling revenue less than 33%? Is the property free of marijuana/hemp activity?
- ☐ Equity: Do you have verified cash equal to 10% of the Total Project Cost?
- ☐ Occupancy: Will you occupy at least 51% of the building (60% for new construction)?

- ☐ Environmental: Is the property free of environmental contamination (dry cleaners, gas stations)?

If you checked all the boxes, congratulations. You have passed the first major hurdle. You are eligible. Now, we must determine if you are creditworthy. That brings us to Chapter 3: The Cash Flow Analysis.

CHAPTER 3

# WHICH SBA LOAN PROGRAM FITS YOUR HOTEL NEEDS?

Here's the truth about SBA hotel financing that nobody tells you: choosing the wrong loan program will cost you tens of thousands of dollars over the life of your loan. Most people assume all SBA loans are the same. They're not. The decision you make in this chapter will affect every payment you make for the next 25 years.

## I. Introduction: Two Paths to Hotel Ownership

You have identified the property: a roadside motel with good bones that needs new management, or maybe a tired independent hotel that you plan to convert into a top-tier franchise. You have the vision, and you have run the numbers on the Average Daily Rate (ADR) and Revenue Per Available Room (RevPAR). Now you face the most critical decision in the financing process.

Which loan program do you choose?

For most small business owners, "SBA financing" is a generic term. They assume there is a single government line of credit. In reality, the Small Business Administration offers two distinct primary vehicles for hotel financing: the 7(a) Loan Program and the 504

Loan Program. Choosing the wrong one is not a matter of paying a slightly higher interest rate. It can kill your deal entirely.

The "best" loan is not simply the one with the lowest rate. It is the one that matches your specific project needs, your available cash (equity), and your long-term goals.

To make this practical, we will continue following Raj and Anil as they choose the right loan program for their situations.

**Raj's deal:**

- Purchase Price: $1.8 million.
- Available Equity: $180,000 (exactly 10%).
- Goal: buy the motel, keep the name, and streamline operations.

**Anil's deal:**

- Acquisition Price: $1.9 million.
- Renovation (PIP) Budget: $600,000.
- Total Project Cost: $2.5 million.
- Goal: Rebrand the asset to increase ADR and capture loyalty rewards travelers.

**Meet Sarah:**

Sarah owns a successful boutique hotel she purchased five years ago with a conventional bank loan. That loan has a "balloon payment" coming due in six months. She needs to address the balloon payment and wants to refinance into stable, long-term debt while pulling out some cash to expand her wedding venue.

- Appraised Value: $4.2 million.
- Existing Debt: $2.1 million.
- Goal: Refinance out of the balloon note and build a new event pavilion.

Raj, Anil, and Sarah have different needs. One needs maximum use because cash is tight. Another involves a complex renovation and franchising agreement. The third needs to restructure existing debt. By the end of this chapter, you will understand exactly why one of them must use the 7(a) program, while another might benefit significantly from the 504 program.

### The Decision Matrix

Before we examine the technical details, view your decision through this high-level comparison.

**The SBA 7(a) Program is the "Swiss Army Knife."**
It is flexible. It handles everything in one bucket: real estate, goodwill, franchise fees, working capital, inventory, and renovations. It is easier to close, but it usually comes with a variable interest rate and a slightly higher fee structure. It is ideal for operators who need to wrap multiple business costs into a single loan.

**The SBA 504 Program is the "Real Estate Specialist."**
It is a heavy lifter designed specifically for buying fixed assets (land, buildings, and heavy equipment). It offers a below-market fixed interest rate for 20 or 25 years. However, it is rigid. It dislikes "soft costs" (like working capital or franchise fees) and requires a higher down payment for hotel projects.

## II. The 7(a) Loan Program: Versatility for Operators

The 7(a) loan is the most popular SBA loan for a reason. For hotel operators, specifically, it offers a level of flexibility that traditional commercial loans cannot touch. When you are buying a hotel, you are rarely buying a building. You are buying a business, a brand, a customer list, and a future cash flow stream. The 7(a) program recognizes this "business" component better than the 504.

## The Mechanics of the 7(a)

In a 7(a) loan, you work with a single lender (a bank or non-bank lender). That lender provides 100% of the loan amount, and the SBA guarantees a portion of that loan (typically 75%) to protect the lender against default.

**Key Terms for Hoteliers:**

- Maximum Loan Amount: $5 million. This is the maximum loan amount. Note: The SBA guarantees a percentage of the loan (up to 85% for smaller loans, 75% for loans over $150,000), not the full amount. On a $5 million loan, maximum SBA exposure is $3.75 million.
- Maturity: Real estate deals get 25 years. If you are buying a business without real estate (like a leasehold interest), it is 10 years. Most hotel deals are 25 years fully amortized, meaning no balloon payments.
- Interest Rates: Typically variable, based on the Prime Rate plus a margin (e.g., Prime + 1.5% to 2.75%).
- Prepayment Penalty: This is a common point of confusion. For loans with a maturity of 15 years or longer (which includes almost all hotel loans), there is a three-year prepayment penalty. It is 5% in year one, 3% in year two, and 1% in year three. After three years, you can refinance or sell with zero penalty.

## Eligible Uses Specific to Hotels

According to **SOP 50 10 8**, the 7(a) program allows you to use proceeds for a vast array of hotel-specific needs.

**1. Change of Ownership**

This is the standard acquisition. You can use one loan to pay for the land, the building, the beds (FF&E), and the "goodwill" (the value of the business above the asset price). Because hotels often trade based on a multiple of earnings than the brick-and-mortar value, having a loan that covers goodwill is essential.

**2. Property Improvement Plans (PIPs)**
This is where 7(a) performs best. If you are buying a franchise (like a Best Western or Holiday Inn Express), the franchisor will issue a PIP. This is a mandatory list of renovations you must complete, usually within 12 to 24 months. A PIP might cost $500,000.

- The 7(a) Advantage: The 7(a) loan can include the PIP amount in the total loan. You close on the buy, and the lender holds the PIP money in an escrow account, releasing it as you complete the work.
- Soft Costs: PIPs often include "soft costs" like architect fees, permitting, and the first franchise application fee (often $25,000 to $50,000). The 7(a) loan finances these easily.

**3. Working Capital and Inventory**
Hotels are cash-hungry businesses, especially during the off-season. If you purchase a hotel in November in a summer tourist town, you need cash to survive until May.

- 7(a) Flexibility: You can add $100,000 or $200,000 of working capital directly into the loan. You can also finance the first buy of linens, soaps, food and beverage inventory, and housekeeping supplies.

**4. Furniture, Fixtures, and Equipment (FF&E)**
Hotels consume equipment. Mattresses, televisions, and lobby furniture often have a useful life of 5 to 7 years. The 7(a) program allows you to finance these assets. While the 504 program generally requires assets to have a 10-year useful life, the 7(a) allows for

shorter-term assets to be bundled into the main loan or structured as a separate 10-year term loan.

## The Affiliation Trap: A Hidden Limitation

There is a critical limitation to the 7(a) program that affects experienced hoteliers: **Affiliation**.

The $5 million maximum loan amount applies to the *borrower and their affiliates*.

If you own two other hotels with SBA 7(a) loans, and you have already used $4 million of your SBA eligibility, you only have $1 million left. You cannot get a new $5 million loan for a third hotel. The SBA looks at the "common ownership" to determine affiliation. If you own 50% of Hotel A and 50% of Hotel B, they are affiliates.

This is often the deciding factor for experienced owners. Once you max out your $5 million 7(a) limit, you *must* switch to the 504 program or conventional financing for future projects.

What If You Already Have an SBA Loan?

If you already have an SBA loan—whether on another hotel, a restaurant, or a completely different business—you are not disqualified. But there are limits, and lenders will scrutinize your application more carefully.

The Aggregate Guaranty Cap

The SBA limits the total guaranteed amount across all your loans (including those of your affiliates) to $3,750,000. This is not the loan amount—it is the SBA's share.

Example: Anil already has a $2 million SBA loan on his first hotel (75% guaranteed = $1.5 million SBA exposure). He wants a $1.9 million loan for the new property (75% guaranteed = $1.425 million). His total SBA exposure would be $2.925 million—under the cap. He is eligible.

Example: If Anil's existing SBA exposure were $3 million, he would only have $750,000 of guaranty room left. The lender would need to reduce the guaranty percentage or decline the loan.

The 90-Day Rule

If you receive two or more SBA 7(a) loans within 90 days of each other, the SBA treats them as a single loan for two purposes:

1. Guaranty Percentage: The combined loan amount determines the guaranty. If the total exceeds $150,000, the guaranty cannot exceed 75%.
2. Upfront Fees: The fee on the second loan is calculated as if both loans were one, minus the fee already paid on the first.

Why This Matters: If you are acquiring two properties simultaneously, discuss timing with your lender. Spacing closings more than 90 days apart may provide fee and guaranty benefits.

Refinancing Your Existing SBA Loan

You can refinance an existing SBA loan into a new SBA loan, but you must meet specific conditions:

- The existing loan must be current (no payment more than 29 days late) for at least the last 12 months.
- The new installment payment must be at least 10 percent less than the existing payment (unless the old loan has a balloon payment coming due).

## The 7(a) Equity Reality

SBA rules (SOP 50 10 8) technically allow for low equity (or even zero equity) in certain "complete change of ownership" scenarios if the business has strong financials. However, do not rely on this technicality.

**Prudent Lending Standards:**

Almost every bank will require a minimum of **10% equity injection** for a hotel acquisition. For a turnaround project or a projection-based deal (where the hotel is currently losing money), the lender may ask for 15% or 20%. The 7(a) is flexible, but it is not free money.

### Reality Check: The Variable Rate Risk

The biggest downside of the 7(a) for hotel owners is the interest rate. Because it is usually Prime-based, your payment fluctuates. If the Federal Reserve hikes rates, your monthly mortgage payment goes up. For a hotel operating on thin margins, a 2% rate hike can eviscerate your cash flow.

**Pro Tip:** Ask your lender about a "fixed-rate" 7(a). They are rare, but some lenders act as "PLP" (Preferred Lenders) and have the ability to offer fixed rates for 3 or 5 years before they float.

## III. The 504 Loan Program: Advantages for Real Estate

If the 7(a) is the flexible generalist, the 504 is the specialized heavy lifter. It is designed by the SBA specifically to help businesses buy fixed assets like land and buildings to promote economic development.

For hotel owners, the 504 is attractive for two reasons: **Fixed Interest Rates** and **Higher Loan Limits**.

### The Three-Part Structure

The 504 is not one loan. It is three distinct parts that come together to fund your project.

- 50% First Mortgage (The Senior Lien): A bank or credit union lends 50% of the project cost. They get the first lien position. This loan typically has a fixed rate for 5 to 10 years and then adjusts.
- 30% to 40% Second Mortgage (The Junior Lien): This is the "SBA" portion, funded by a Certified Development Company (CDC) through the sale of a debenture (bond) on Wall Street. This portion has a fixed interest rate for 20 or 25 years.
- 10% to 20% Borrower Equity: This is your down payment.

### The Massive Benefit: Long-Term Fixed Rates

The rate on the SBA portion (the debenture) is usually well below market commercial rates. More importantly, it is fixed for 25 years. This provides cost certainty. If you are building a hotel from the ground up, knowing exactly what your mortgage payment will be in year 15 is a massive financial advantage.

### The Interim "Bridge" Loan Process

This is the most complex part of a 504 loan, and it often catches borrowers by surprise.

The SBA portion of the funds (the debenture) is not available at the closing table. The SBA sells these bonds on Wall Street only once a month, and only *after* the project is complete.

**How it works:**

- Closing: The bank funds its 50% portion. You put in your equity. But who pays the remaining 30-40% needed to purchase the seller's building?
- The Bridge: The bank provides an "Interim Loan" (or Bridge Loan) to cover the SBA's portion.
- The Float: You pay interest on this bridge loan (usually interest-only) until the project is finished.
- The Takeout: Once you have the deed (or Certificate of Occupancy for construction), the CDC sells the bond, pays off the bank's bridge loan, and you are left with the two permanent mortgages.

**Why this matters:** You have exposure to interest rate risk during the interim period. Also, you pay closing costs on the bridge loan *and* the permanent loan.

### The Equity Trap: Special Purpose Properties

Here is the catch. While a standard warehouse or office building might qualify for 10% down on a 504 loan, hotels are treated differently.

Under SBA rules (13 CFR 120.910), hotels are classified as **"Special Purpose Properties."** The SBA defines these as properties with a unique design, layout, or construction that restricts their utility for other purposes. You cannot easily turn a hotel into an office building without gutting it.

**The "Special Purpose" Penalty:**
Because the collateral is harder to liquidate, the SBA requires an more 5% equity injection from the borrower.

- Standard 504 Equity: 10%
- Hotel 504 Equity: 15%

**The "New Business" Penalty:**
The SBA defines a "New Business" as one in operation for 2 years or less. However, **SBA Procedural Notice 5000-872764** clarifies that if there is a change of ownership resulting in new, unproven management, it may be classified as a New Business even if the building has been a motel for 40 years.

If you are a New Business buying a Special Purpose Property (Hotel), the SBA requires **another 5% equity injection**.

**The Total Down Payment:**
If you are a first-time buyer (New Business) buying a hotel (Special Purpose):

- Base: 10%
- Special Purpose: +5%
- New Business: +5%
- Total Equity Required: 20%

This 20% requirement is the single biggest barrier for entry-level hoteliers looking at the 504 program.

## The "Green" 504: Breaking the Cap

Normally, the SBA 504 portion is capped at $5 million (or $5.5 million for manufacturers). However, there is a powerful exception called the **Energy Public Policy Goal** (or "Green 504").

If your hotel project reduces energy consumption by 10% (for an existing building) or generates 15% of its energy from renewable sources (like solar panels), you gain two benefits:

- Higher Cap: The SBA lending limit increases to $5.5 million per project.
- Aggregate Exception: The $16.5 million aggregate limit applies per project. You could theoretically finance multiple $15 million hotel projects using the Green 504, provided each one meets the energy goals.

This is the secret weapon for large-scale hotel developers who want to use SBA financing for multiple properties.

## Eligible Uses and Restrictions

The 504 is strict about what the money buys.

- Eligible: Land buy, building acquisition, ground-up construction, heavy renovations (new roof, HVAC, structural changes), and heavy equipment with a useful life of 10+ years (like commercial laundry systems or kitchen hoods).
- Ineligible: Working capital, inventory (linens/food), franchise fees, marketing costs, and goodwill.

Reality Check: If you purchase a hotel for $5 million, but the appraisal says the building is worth $4 million and the business value (goodwill) is $1 million, the 504 program struggles. The 504 can only finance the fixed assets. You would have to pay the $1 million goodwill out of pocket or find a lender willing to structure a separate side loan (which is messy and often disallowed).

## IV. Hotel-Specific Requirements

Hotel financing sits at the intersection of real estate law and business operations. Regardless of whether you choose 7(a) or 504, you must clear these specific "tripwires."

### Occupancy Rules and Third-Party Tenants

The SBA requires you to "occupy" the building. You cannot use SBA money to purchase a building and rent it out to others (that is for investment landlords, not small business owners).

**The Rules (13 CFR 120.131):**

- Existing Buildings: You must occupy at least 51% of the rentable square footage.
- New Construction: You must occupy at least 60% initially, moving to 80% within 10 years.

**The Hotel Trap:**

Hotels often have third-party tenants: a restaurant on the ground floor, a spa leased to an operator, or a gift shop.

- *Scenario:* You buy a hotel with 50,000 square feet. There is a steakhouse attached that leases 20,000 square feet.
- *Calculation:* You occupy 30,000 sq ft (60%). The tenant occupies 20,000 sq ft (40%). This works.
- *Scenario:* You buy a mixed-use building with a small boutique hotel upstairs (4,000 sq ft) and a massive retail space downstairs (5,000 sq ft) that you lease out.
- *Calculation:* You occupy 44%. This deal is ineligible.

### The Franchise Directory and Comfort Letter

If you are flagging your hotel (Marriott, Hilton, IHG, Choice, Wyndham), the SBA must approve the franchise agreement.

The Directory: Check that your brand is on the SBA Franchise

Directory. If listed, you're clear. If not, the SBA must review the Franchise Disclosure Document (FDD), adding weeks to the process.

The Comfort Letter: This is the document that causes the most delays in hotel lending. It is a tri-party agreement between the Bank, the SBA, and the Franchisor. It essentially states that if you default on your loan, the Franchisor will allow the Bank to step in and operate the hotel (or sell it) without losing the flag now.

- *Warning:* Large franchisors like Marriott and Hilton are notoriously slow at signing these. Start this process the day you sign your purchase contract.

## The PIP Funding Gap

We mentioned PIPs earlier, but here is the technical mismatch with the 504 loan.

A PIP budget usually looks like this:

- Hard Construction (Flooring, Paint, Wall movement): $300,000
- FF&E (Furniture, Beds, TVs): $150,000
- Soft Costs (Design, Architect, Permits): $50,000

**7(a) Loan:** Covers all $500,000.

504 Loan: Covers the $300,000 construction. It might cover the furniture *if* you can prove a 10-year useful life (hard for beds). It generally rejects the soft costs.

- Result: In a 504 deal, you likely have to pay the soft costs and some FF&E out of pocket, increasing your cash to close.

## Life Insurance Requirements

Be prepared for a personal requirement: Life Insurance.

Under SOP 50 10 8, lenders must require life insurance on the key business owners if the loan is not fully secured by collateral.

Since hotel loans often use high Loan-to-Value (LTV) ratios, there is almost always a collateral shortfall.

- You will need to assign a life insurance policy to the lender for the amount of the loan. If you have a pre-existing condition that makes you uninsurable, this can stop a loan approval. Discuss this early.

## V. Advanced Strategy: Refinancing

Refinancing is the third common scenario (like our borrower Sarah). The rules for refinancing SBA debt are specific and favorable for hoteliers trapped in high-interest or ballooning debt.

### A. 7(a) Debt Refinancing

You can use a 7(a) loan to refinance existing commercial debt (even from another bank) if:

- Substantial Benefit: The new loan payment must be at least 10% lower than your current payment.
- Current Status: You must have been current on the debt for the last 12 months. No 30-day lates.
- Balloon: If your current loan has a balloon payment (like Sarah's), you automatically qualify to refinance it, even if the payment reduction isn't 10%.

### B. 504 Debt Refinancing With Expansion

This allows you to refinance existing debt *and* get money for a new project (Expansion).

- The Rule: If you are building a new wing (Expansion) that costs $1 million, you can refinance up to $1 million of existing debt into the 504 loan.
- Limit: The debt refinance amount cannot exceed 100% of the expansion cost.

### C. 504 Debt Refinancing Without Expansion

This is a pure refinance product introduced to help stable businesses lock in long-term rates.

- Eligibility: The business must have been in operation for 2 years.
- LTV Limit: The Loan-to-Value is capped at 90%.
- Qualified Debt: The debt must be at least 6 months old and substantially (85%) used for eligible fixed assets (land/building). You cannot use this to refinance a line of credit used for payroll.

## VI. Comparative Analysis: Matching Program to Project

Now that we understand the mechanics, let us compare the two programs side-by-side.

| Feature | SBA 7(a) Loan | SBA 504 Loan |
|---|---|---|
| Max Loan Amount | $5 Million (SBA Portion) | Unlimited (Bank) + $5.5M (SBA) |
| Interest Rate | Variable (Prime + Margin) | Fixed (SBA portion is fixed 20/25 yrs) |
| Down Payment (Equity) | Typically 10-15% | 15% (Experienced) or 20% (New) |
| Use of Proceeds | Real Estate, PIP, Goodwill, Working Cap | Real Estate & Heavy Equipment Only |
| Soft Costs | Eligible | Limited / Ineligible |
| Goodwill | Eligible | Ineligible |
| Fees | Guaranty Fee (based on loan size) | Participation Fee + Debenture Fees |
| Prepayment Penalty | 3 Years (5% / 3% / 1%) | 10 Years (Declining balance) |

| | | |
|---|---|---|
| Closing Speed | Faster (45-60 days) | Slower (60-90 days) due to 2 lenders |
| Collateral | All business assets + Real Estate | Real Estate & Fixed Assets |

## Project Matching Guide

**1. Acquisition of Operating Hotel**

- Use 7(a) if: You have low equity (10%), the price includes significant goodwill, or you need working capital.
- Use 504 if: You have high equity (15-20%), the value is mostly real estate, and the project is over $5 million.

**2. Renovation / PIP**

- Use 7(a) if: The PIP involves soft costs, short-term assets (linens/TVs), or franchise fees.
- Use 504 if: The renovation is massive (gut rehab, new roof, structural) and exceeds the value of soft costs significantly.

**3. New Construction**

- Use 504 if: You want to lock in a fixed rate for 25 years on a large asset. The protection against rising rates is invaluable for new builds.
- Use 7(a) if: The project is smaller (<$5M) and you want a simpler "one-closing" process without managing a bridge loan.

## VII. Case Studies: Raj, Anil, and Sarah

Let us return to our borrowers to see how these rules dictate their financial destiny.

## A. Case Study 1: Raj (The First-Time Buyer)

**The Scenario:**

Raj is acquiring a 40-room independent highway motel.

- Price: $1.8 million.
- Equity Available: $180,000.
- Status: First-time buyer (New Business).
- Property Type: Special Purpose (Hotel).

**The 504 Analysis (Failure):**

If Raj approaches a CDC for a 504 loan, here is the math:

- Special Purpose Rule: Hotels require +5% equity.
- New Business Rule: Raj is a new operator. This triggers another +5% equity.
- Calculation: 10% (Base) + 5% (Hotel) + 5% (New) = 20% Total Equity.
- Requirement: 20% of $1.8M = $360,000.
- Result: Raj only has $180,000. He is short by $180,000. The 504 loan is mathematically impossible for him unless he brings in a partner.

**The 7(a) Analysis (Success):**

- Equity Rule: The 7(a) lender accepts 10% equity ($180,000).
- Working Capital: Raj needs $50,000 for the first winter. The 7(a) lender adds this to the loan amount.
- Result: Raj qualifies. He accepts the variable interest rate because it is the only vehicle that allows him to purchase the property with his available cash.

**Verdict for Raj: SBA 7(a).**

## B. Case Study 2: Anil (The Experienced Conversion)

**The Scenario:**

Anil is acquiring a 55-room motel to convert to a Choice Hotels flag.

- Acquisition Price: $1.9 million.
- PIP Renovation: $600,000.
- Total Project: $2.5 million.
- Status: Experienced operator (owns 2 other properties).
- Equity Available: $500,000 (20%).

**The 504 Analysis (Possible but Rigid):**

- Equity: As an experienced operator, Anil avoids the "New Business" penalty. He only faces the "Special Purpose" rule (15%). He has 20% cash, so he qualifies on equity.
- The PIP Problem: The CDC reviews the $600,000 PIP budget.
  - $400,000 is Hard Costs (Construction, HVAC). Eligible.
  - $100,000 is Short-term FF&E (Mattresses, small furniture). Likely Ineligible.
  - $50,000 is Franchise Fee. Ineligible.
  - $50,000 is Marketing/Soft Costs. Ineligible.
- Result: Anil must pay the $200,000 in ineligible costs *out of pocket* in addition to his 15% down payment ($375,000). Total cash needed: $575,000. He only has $500,000. The deal fails on liquidity.

**The 7(a) Analysis (Preferred):**

- Loan Structure: The lender bundles the acquisition ($1.9M) and the full PIP ($600K) including the franchise fees and marketing.

- Simplicity: Anil closes one loan. The lender sets aside the $600k in an escrow account.
- Equity: Anil puts down 15% of the *total* project ($375,000).
- Result: Anil has $125,000 remaining in cash reserves for operational emergencies.

**Verdict for Anil: SBA 7(a).**

## C. Case Study 3: Sarah (The Refinance)

**The Scenario:**
Sarah owns a boutique hotel with a balloon payment due.

- Appraised Value: $4.2 million.
- Existing Debt: $2.1 million.
- Expansion Cost: $1.5 million (New Pavilion).
- Total Debt Need: $3.6 million.
- LTV: 85%.

**The 7(a) Analysis (Limited):**
Sarah could use 7(a), but the variable rate exposes her to risk. Also, if she already has other SBA loans, the $3.6 million might push her close to the $5 million cap.

**The 504 Analysis (Superior):**

- Refi with Expansion: Sarah is building a $1.5 million pavilion. The rules allow her to refinance up to 100% of the expansion cost ($1.5M) of existing debt.
- Wait, she has $2.1M debt: The "Refi with Expansion" rule only covers $1.5M of the old debt. This specific rule doesn't fit her full need.

- Better Option: Refi Without Expansion: Since her hotel is 5 years old (Operating Business > 2 years), she can use the "Refi Without Expansion" program.
- LTV: She is at 85% LTV ($3.6M / $4.2M). The program allows up to 90%.
- Benefit: She locks in a 25-year fixed rate on the SBA portion. She eliminates the balloon payment risk forever.

**Verdict for Sarah: SBA 504 (Refinance Program).**

## VIII. Summary Checklist: Making Your Choice

When you sit down with your loan broker or banker, have this checklist ready to guide the conversation.

**1. Equity Check**

☐ Do I have exactly 10% of the total project cost? -> Focus on 7(a).
☐ Do I have 15% to 20% available? -> Consider 504.

**2. Use of Proceeds**

☐ Is the deal mostly real estate (land/building)? -> 504 is strong.
☐ Is there significant "Goodwill" (business value) in the price? -> 7(a) is better.
☐ Is there a PIP with significant soft costs or short-life assets? -> 7(a) is better.
☐ Do I need working capital included in the loan? -> 7(a) is required.

**3. Affiliation and Limits**

☐ Do I own other hotels with SBA debt?
☐ Will this loan push my total SBA aggregate over $5 million? -> If yes, you MUST use 504.

**4. Interest Rate Tolerance**

☐ Can I handle a variable rate if it goes up 2%? -> 7(a) is acceptable.

☐ Do I need a fixed payment to sleep at night? -> 504 is preferred.

Hotel financing is complex because the asset is both real estate and an operating business. By understanding the constraints of equity, the nature of your renovation plans, and the affiliation rules, you can stop guessing and choose the vehicle that gets you to the closing table.

In the next chapter, we will discuss exactly how to prepare the specific documents a hotel lender needs—including the all-important STR report and Star Report analysis.

Disclaimer: *I am a guide writer, not a lending officer or attorney. SBA rules (SOP 50 10 8) are subject to change. Always verify current equity requirements, affiliation rules, and eligibility with a qualified SBA lender or CDC before signing purchase agreements.*

**Sources:**


- SOP 50 10 8, Section B, Chapter 1 (Standard 7(a) Loans).
- SOP 50 10 8, Section C, Chapter 1 (504 Loans - Eligibility and Equity).
- 13 CFR § 120.882 (Eligible Project Costs for 504).
- 13 CFR § 120.131 (Leasing Requirements).
- SBA Procedural Notice 5000-872764 (New Business Definition).


Now that you know which loan program fits your deal, the next question is: how do you actually apply? The application process is where good deals go to die—or where prepared borrowers separate themselves from the pack.

## CHAPTER 4

# THE APPLICATION PROCESS WHAT TO EXPECT

Now that you understand which loan program fits your project, here's the thing about SBA applications that nobody tells you: the biggest mistake hotel buyers make is treating this like a regular bank loan. You've done the hard work—found the property, confirmed eligibility, chosen your program. Now comes the test that separates funded deals from failed dreams.

You have defined your project. You have identified the property. Now you face the most rigorous phase of SBA lending: the application.

You might view the application as a single form or a stack of papers to sign. This misconception leads to frustration. The SBA application is not a single event. It is a process of forensic discovery. The lender, acting as an agent for the federal government, must construct a file that proves three things: you are eligible, you can repay the loan, and the government's risk is minimized.

For hotel buyers like Raj and experienced operators like Anil, this process has specific requirements that generic businesses do not face. You are not buying a building. You are buying a "Special

Purpose Property" that functions as an operating business. The scrutiny is higher, the documentation is heavier, and the timeline is stricter.

This chapter breaks down the application process from the first handshake to the issuance of the E-Tran Terms and Conditions and the final closing steps. We will walk through the specific requirements for independent motels and franchised hotels, how to handle equity injection, the hidden costs of applying, and how to manage the timeline so you do not lose your purchase contract.

## I. Preparation and Lender Selection

Before you fill out a single government form, you must find the right partner. The SBA does not lend money directly to you. Banks and non-bank lenders lend the money. The SBA guarantees a portion of that loan (usually 75 percent) to protect the lender if you default.

Because the lender takes the risk (25 percent of it, anyway), the lender makes the decision. However, not all lenders interpret SBA rules the same way, and not all lenders understand the hospitality industry.

### A. Finding Hotel-Experienced Lenders

The SBA Standard Operating Procedures (SOP 50 10 8) classify hotels, motels, and lodging facilities as "Limited or Special Purpose Properties." This is a significant distinction. A warehouse can be converted into a gym or a storage facility. A 40-room motel is difficult to convert into anything else without massive expense.

Because the collateral is specialized, the lender must have experience in valuing and liquidating hotels. If you apply with a local community bank that mostly finances car washes or dental practices, you may face rejection not because your deal is bad, but because the bank does not understand the hotel business model.

**The PLP Distinction**

You will hear the term "PLP" often. It stands for Preferred Lenders Program.

- PLP Lenders: These banks have "delegated authority." The SBA has given them the power to approve the loan on behalf of the government. They do not send your file to the SBA for a credit decision. They make the decision in-house. This saves weeks of processing time.
- Standard (Non-Delegated) Lenders: These lenders must package your application and send it to the SBA's Loan Guaranty Processing Center (LGPC). An SBA loan officer reviews the file and makes the final decision.

**Scenario: Raj's Lender Choice**

Raj is buying a 40-room independent motel for $1.8 million. He walks into the local branch of a major national bank where he keeps his personal checking account. He assumes his loyalty will help.

- *The Outcome:* The branch manager takes his information but eventually declines the loan. The big bank views independent motels in rural areas as "high risk" and prefers franchised properties in urban centers. Raj wasted three weeks.
- *The Pivot:* Raj connects with a PLP lender who specializes in hospitality. This lender understands that independent motels have lower overhead costs (no royalty fees) and can be highly profitable. They are willing to look at the deal under delegated authority.

## B. The Letter of Intent (LOI) and Pre-Qualification

The process formally begins when you submit preliminary financial data to a lender to get a Term Sheet or Letter of Intent (LOI). This is not a binding loan approval. It is an expression of interest.

To get this, you need to provide:

- Personal Financial Statement (PFS): A snapshot of what you own and what you owe.
- Seller's Financials: Three years of tax returns and a current Profit & Loss statement for the hotel you are buying.
- The Deal Structure: purchase price, renovation costs, and your proposed down payment.

Reality Check: Lenders will issue a "soft quote" quickly. Do not celebrate yet. A soft quote assumes everything you told them is 100 percent accurate and that the property appraisal will match the purchase price. The hard work starts after you sign this LOI.

## C. Sizing the Deal: Fees and Real Costs

Before you commit to a lender, you must understand the cost of admission. The "down payment" is not your only cash requirement. You must budget for the **SBA Guaranty Fee** and the **Lender Packaging Fee**.

### 1. The SBA Guaranty Fee

This is a fee charged by the federal government. It is not negotiable. For most hotel loans (which usually exceed $1 million), the fee is substantial. The fee is calculated on the *guaranteed* portion of the loan, not the total loan amount.

As of the current fiscal year, the fee structure is tiered (Source 30):

- Loans up to $1 million: 0 percent fee (subject to fiscal year changes).
- Loans over $1 million: A tiered calculation that can reach up to 3.75 percent of the guaranteed portion.

**Example Calculation:**

Raj is borrowing $1.6 million. The SBA guarantees 75 percent ($1.2 million).

- The fee is 3.5% on the $700,001-$1M portion and 3.75% on amounts over $1M of that $1.2 million.
- Raj will owe $42,500 in Guaranty Fees (3.5% on the first $1M of the guaranteed portion = $35,000, plus 3.75% on the remaining $200,000 = $7,500).

*Pro Tip:* You can finance this fee into the loan amount, but it increases your monthly debt service.

**2. Lender Packaging Fee**

The lender is allowed to charge a fee for packaging the loan application.

- SBA Form 159 (Fee Disclosure): You will sign this form at closing. It discloses exactly who was paid what.
- The Limit: The lender can charge a reasonable fee, often between $2,500 and $5,000. If a consultant or broker introduces you to the bank, their fee also appears on Form 159. Be wary of brokers asking for upfront fees before an LOI is issued. Legitimate lenders and brokers get paid when the loan closes.

## II. The Application Package: Core Documentation

Once you accept the lender's Term Sheet, you enter the underwriting phase. The lender will send you a "Needs List" that can run five pages long. Do not be intimidated. We will categorize these into three buckets: Core Forms, Financial Proof, and Deal Specifics.

### A. Core SBA Forms

These are the federal documents required for every SBA 7(a) loan.

**1. SBA Form 1919 (Borrower Information Form)**
This is the primary application form. It asks for your personal information, the business structure, and answers to legal questions (criminal history, citizenship, other government debt).

- Citizenship and Ownership (PN 5000-876441, effective March 1, 2026): The SBA has strict rules about ownership. You must attest that 100 percent of the owners are U.S. Citizens or U.S. Nationals with Principal Residence in the United States, its territories, or possessions. Note: Lawful Permanent Residents (Green Card holders) are no longer eligible.
    * *No Foreign Ownership Exception (March 1, 2026):* The previous 5% exception has been eliminated. Any foreign national ownership-even 1%-makes the loan ineligible. If you have a cousin in India who wants to invest $50,000 for a 10 percent share, the loan will be ineligible unless he has a Green Card.
- Who Signs? Every owner with 20 percent or more equity must sign this form. If you own 100 percent, only you sign. If Raj and his wife own 50 percent each, both must complete a Form 1919.

**2. SBA Form 1919 (Statement of Personal History)**
This form causes more anxiety than any other document. It asks about your criminal history.

- The Question: "Have you ever been arrested, prosecuted, or convicted of a crime?"
- The Trap: Many borrowers answer "No" because they had a charge dismissed 20 years ago or expunged. The FBI background check sees everything. If you answer "No" and the FBI report says "Yes," you will be declined for "lack of candor."

- Moral Turpitude: If you have a prior offense, the lender must determine if it is a "crime of moral turpitude." A DUI is generally not moral turpitude (though multiple DUIs suggest a character issue). Fraud, theft, or assault are crimes of moral turpitude.
- The Fingerprint Process: If you answer "Yes" to questions about criminal history, you must submit a detailed explanation and court documents. The lender may need to submit your fingerprints to the FBI for a background check. This adds 2 to 4 weeks to the timeline.

**Pro Tip:** Be honest. Disclose the college prank from 1998. It is rarely a deal-killer if disclosed. It is always a deal-killer if hidden.

**3. SBA Form 413 (Personal Financial Statement)**

This form gives the lender a look at your personal stability. You must list every asset (cash, retirement accounts, real estate) and every liability (mortgages, credit cards, student loans).

- Joint Assets: If you are married, you must include your spouse's assets and liabilities, even if your spouse is not on the loan. The SBA needs to know the total household financial picture to ensure you aren't hiding liabilities under a spouse's name.
- Signature: Your spouse must sign this form to acknowledge the assets are being disclosed, even if they are not guaranteeing the loan.
- Accuracy Warning: Do not list your hotel's revenue as your personal income. That is a common mistake. Your income is the salary or draw you take from the business.

### B. Financial Documentation

The lender needs to calculate two things: Historical Cash Flow (can the business pay the loan based on past performance?) and Global Cash Flow (can you pay your personal bills and the business debt?).

**1. Historical Data (The Seller)**

For Raj's acquisition, he needs the seller's tax returns for the last three years.

- *The Interim Statement:* If the tax return is for last year, and it is now July, Raj needs an "Interim P&L" for January through June. SBA rules require financials dated within 120 days of submission.
- *Verification (Form 4506-C):* The lender will have Raj sign an IRS Form 4506-C. This allows the lender to pull a transcript directly from the IRS. This forensic step ensures the tax returns given by the seller match what was filed with the government. If the seller gave Raj "management books" showing higher income than the tax returns, the lender will ignore the management books. The SBA lends on tax-verified income only.

**2. The Debt Schedule**

This is a list of every business debt the entity currently owes or will owe. Since Raj is buying the assets free and clear, his debt schedule will be simple: the new SBA loan.

For Anil, who owns two other hotels, this is complex. He must list the mortgages on his other properties. The lender will perform a "Global Cash Flow Analysis." They need to ensure Anil isn't bleeding cash at his other hotels, which would threaten the new project.

**3. Debt Refinancing Rules (The "Same Institution" Trap)**

Many hotel applications involve refinancing existing debt to get a lower rate or a longer term.

- The Rule: If you are refinancing a loan, you must prove the new loan provides a "substantial benefit" (usually a 10 percent reduction in payments).
- The Same Institution Debt (SID) Restriction: If you apply to Bank A to refinance a loan you already have with Bank

A, Bank A *cannot* use its PLP (delegated) authority (Source 24). They must send the file to the SBA for non-delegated review. This is to prevent banks from dumping their bad loans onto the SBA guarantee.

- *Action:* If you need to refinance a loan, it is often faster to move to a *new* lender who can use PLP authority to pay off the old bank.

**4. Projections (The Pro Forma)**

Projections are your estimate of future performance.

- When are they required? You must provide projections if you are a "New Business" (startup), or if the historical cash flow doesn't support the loan (turnaround situations), or if you are expanding (Anil's conversion).
- The Raj Scenario (New Management): Raj is buying an operating motel, but he has never owned it. The lender may require a month-by-month projection for the first year to prove Raj understands the seasonality. If the motel is near a ski resort, revenue might be zero in July. Raj's projection must reflect that.
- The Anil Scenario (Change of Flag): Anil is spending $600,000 to renovate. He cannot rely on the old budget motel numbers. He must submit a projection that shows:

* RevPAR Increase: How much will the daily rate increase with the Choice Hotels brand?

* Expense Increase: Franchises charge royalty fees (usually 8 to 12 percent of gross room revenue). Anil's projections must deduct these fees. If he forgets them, the lender will reject the projection as unrealistic.

## C. Deal-Specific Documents

**1. The Purchase Agreement (PSA)**

You must submit the fully signed Purchase and Sale Agreement. It must explicitly state what is being bought: land, building, furniture, fixtures, equipment (FF&E), and goodwill.

- Allocation of Price: The contract should break down the price. $1.5M for Real Estate, $200K for FF&E, $100K for Goodwill. This allocation is vital for the appraisal and the SBA Form 1920.

**2. Business Valuation vs. Real Estate Appraisal**

Hotel loans are unique because a hotel is a business wrapped in real estate. The lender will order a Real Estate Appraisal.

- The Valuation Gap: Sometimes, the real estate (bricks and dirt) is worth $1.5 million, but you are paying $1.8 million because the business generates high cash flow.
- Business Valuation: If the price exceeds the real estate value, the lender must justify the difference as "Goodwill" or "Intangible Assets."
- SBA Form 1920 Requirement: The lender must document the value of the business. If the amount financed for intangible assets exceeds $250,000, the lender generally requires a formal Business Valuation from a qualified source, separate from the real estate appraisal (Source 38).
- Why This Matters: If the appraisal comes in low on the real estate, the deal isn't dead, but the lender must be able to support the remaining value through the business cash flow. If they can't, you may have to lower the purchase price or bring more cash.

**3. Environmental Reports**

Because hotels handle chemicals (pool chlorine, cleaning supplies) and often have old laundry facilities, environmental risk is real.

- Phase I ESA: Most lenders require a Phase I Environmental Site Assessment. An engineer visits the site to check for contamination.
- RSRA: For smaller, lower-risk properties, a "Records Search with Risk Assessment" might suffice. This is faster and cheaper.
- The Dry Cleaner Trap: If Raj's motel is next door to a dry cleaner that has been there for 20 years, the Phase I will likely flag a "Recognized Environmental Condition" (REC) about groundwater contamination. This can kill a deal or require a Phase II (drilling soil samples), which costs thousands of dollars and takes weeks.

## III. Franchise Approval Coordination

If you are buying a franchise (like Anil), or if the property is currently a franchise, the SBA has specific hurdles about the brand.

### A. The SBA Franchise Directory

First, confirm your brand is on the SBA Franchise Directory.

- Mandatory Check: The lender *must* check if the brand is on this list.
- Identifier Code: Each approved brand has a code. For Choice Hotels, there is a code. For Subway, there is a code. The lender enters this code into the SBA E-Tran system.

**The "Off-Directory" Nuance**

What happens if the brand is not on the list?

- Delegated (PLP) Lenders: A PLP lender *cannot* approve a loan for a brand not on the directory using their delegated authority. They are stuck.
- Non-Delegated Processing: However, the deal is not necessarily dead. The lender can submit the franchise agreement and the application to the SBA Loan Guaranty Processing Center (LGPC) for a manual review (Source 1/46). The SBA Franchise Team will review the agreement to ensure the franchisor doesn't exert too much control over you (affiliation issues).
- The Delay: This manual review adds significant time. If you are considering a new or obscure hotel brand, check the directory early. If it's not there, warn your lender now.

**Scenario: The Off-Directory Brand**
Anil considers a smaller, up-and-coming boutique hotel brand called "HipSleep." He checks the SBA Directory and HipSleep is not listed.

- *Action:* Anil must contact the franchisor now. The franchisor needs to submit their documents to the SBA Franchise Team to get added. If Anil applies for the loan before the brand is added, he loses the speed of PLP processing.

## B. Reviewing the Agreements

**1. The Franchise Disclosure Document (FDD)**
The lender will ask for the FDD and the specific Franchise Agreement you signed.

- Term Matching: The term of the franchise agreement must generally match or exceed the term of the loan. If Anil is getting a 25-year SBA loan, but his franchise agreement expires in 10 years, the lender will view this as a risk.

What happens in year 11? Anil may need to negotiate a longer term or renewal options with the franchisor.

**2. Comfort Letters**

This is a tri-party agreement between the Franchisor, the Lender, and You.

- What it says: If you default on the loan, the Franchisor agrees to let the Lender take over the property and sell it as a franchised hotel. Without this, the Franchisor could strip the "flag" now upon default, destroying the hotel's value.
- SBA Form 2462: The SBA has a standard addendum for this. Franchisors on the Directory have already agreed to use the SBA's addendum or a negotiated version.

## IV. Construction and PIP Mechanics

For Anil, the $600,000 renovation is not a cosmetic wish list. It is a mandate from the franchisor known as a Property Improvement Plan (PIP). You might assume the bank will hand them a check for $600,000 at closing. This is incorrect.

### A. Controlling the Cash

The SBA requires lenders to strictly monitor construction funds to ensure the money goes into the building.

- No Cash at Closing: The $600,000 will be placed in a "Construction Escrow" account held by the bank.
- Draw Process: As your contractor completes work (e.g., finishes the bathroom tiling), they submit an invoice. The bank (or a third-party inspector) verifies the work is done. Then, the bank releases the funds directly to the contractor or to you for reimbursement.

- SBA Form 601 (Agreement of Compliance): You and the contractor may need to sign this form. It ensures there are no kickbacks or undisclosed fees in the construction contract.

### B. Contingencies

Lenders know that renovations always cost more than expected.

- The 10 Percent Buffer: The lender will likely require a 10 percent contingency fund added to the construction budget. If the PIP is $600,000, the budget becomes $660,000.

Important: If construction costs exceed first estimates, the SBA loan can sometimes be increased during construction up to the program limit. Discuss this option with your lender early if you encounter cost overruns. Note that an more upfront guarantee fee applies to any increased amount.

- Source of Contingency: You might have to fund this contingency with your own cash, or if the appraisal supports it, the loan can cover it.

## V. Underwriting and "What to Expect" about Equity

Once documents are submitted, the lender's underwriting team goes to work. They are writing a "Credit Memorandum"—essentially a book report on why you are a good risk. The biggest friction point in this phase is Equity Injection.

### A. Equity Injection Requirements

SBA rules on equity are strict. They want you to have "skin in the game."

**1. The Definition of "New Business" (Source 10)**

The SBA recently updated how it defines a "New Business," which impacts your down payment.

- The Old Rule: Any change of ownership was often treated like a startup.
- The New Rule: A business is a "New Business" if it has been in operation for 2 years or less. However, if a business has been operating for *more* than 2 years (like the motel Raj is buying), it is considered a New Business only if the change of ownership results in new, unproven management AND increased debt unrelated to business operations.
- Impact on Raj: Raj is new to the industry. He is unproven. Therefore, the transaction is treated as a New Business. The SBA requires him to inject at least 10 percent of the Total Project Cost.
- Impact on Anil: Anil is an experienced operator expanding his portfolio. He is "proven management." Technically, the SBA minimum equity injection for him could be 10 percent.

* *Reality Check:* While the SBA allows 10 percent, almost no lender will approve a hotel loan with zero down. Lender policy usually dictates a minimum of 10 percent to 15 percent, even for experienced borrowers, to mitigate risk.

**2. Calculating the Injection**

The 10 percent is calculated on the Total Project Cost, not the purchase price.

- Purchase Price: $1.8M
- Closing Costs/Fees: $50,000
- Renovations/PIP: $50,000
- Working Capital: $50,000
- *Total Project:* $1.95M

- *Required Equity (10%):* $195,000.

**3. Source of Funds Verification**

You cannot borrow your down payment. The SBA requires the equity to be your own cash.

- Seasoning: The lender will ask for two months of bank statements. If Raj's balance was $10,000 two months ago and is $195,000 today, the lender will ask: "Where did the $185,000 come from?"
- Acceptable Sources:
  - Savings (verified by statements).
  - HELOC (Home Equity Line of Credit) on a personal residence is allowed *only if* you have an outside income source (like a spouse's salary) to repay the HELOC independent of the hotel's profit.
  - Gift: A parent can gift funds, but they must sign a "Gift Letter" stating the money does not need to be repaid.
- Unacceptable Sources:
  - A loan from a friend that you promised to pay back when the hotel makes money.
  - Cash that cannot be traced (mattress money).

## B. Credit Standards and Ratios

The underwriter focuses on one metric above all others: The Debt Service Coverage Ratio (DSCR).

**The Formula:**

Net Operating Income / Annual Debt Payments`

The SBA minimum is **1.15**. This means for every $1.00 of debt payment, the hotel must generate $1.15 in cash.

- Raj's Math: If the new loan payment is $150,000 per year, the motel must generate $172,500 in Net Operating Income (NOI) after all expenses and Raj's salary.
- The Cushion: Most lenders prefer a DSCR of 1.25 or higher. If the historical tax returns show a DSCR of 0.9 (meaning the hotel lost money), Raj relies entirely on his projections and management plan to prove he can turn it around.

Credit Underwriting for Small vs. Standard Loans (Updated March 1, 2026)

For small loans, lenders now use their own credit analysis processes (PN 5000-875701, effective March 1, 2026). The previous FICO SBSS scoring requirement has been discontinued.

- Loans under $500,000 (SBA Small): As of March 1, 2026, the SBSS requirement is discontinued. Lenders now use their own credit analysis processes. Previously, if your SBSS score was below the lender's cutoff (usually 155-160), the application may be auto-declined or require manual override.
- Loans over $500,000 (Standard 7(a)): For most hotel deals, the loan exceeds $500,000. Note: The SBSS requirement for smaller loans was discontinued March 1, 2026 (PN 5000-875701). For larger loans, the lender uses the SBSS score, but a low score does not automatically kill the deal. The lender can use "traditional underwriting" (analyzing your cash flow and experience) to justify the loan even if the computer score is low (Source 25). Do not panic if your score is 150, provided your cash flow is strong.

## VI. The Approval Timeline

How long does this take? In a perfect world, 45 to 60 days. In reality, often 75 to 90 days.

### A. E-Tran Submission and Authorization

Once the lender finishes the Credit Memo, they enter the data into **E-Tran**, the SBA's electronic system.

- Delegated (PLP) Timeline:
  * Lender Underwriting: 2–4 weeks.
  * SBA Approval: Instant. Once the lender hits "Submit" in E-Tran, an SBA Loan Number is generated.
- Non-Delegated Timeline:
  * Lender Underwriting: 2–4 weeks.
  * SBA LGPC Review: The lender uploads the file to the SBA. The SBA takes 5 to 10 business days to review. If they have questions, the clock stops until the lender answers.

### B. The Terms and Conditions Sheet (The "Ticket")

Approval comes in the form of the **E-Tran Terms and Conditions sheet**. This is a dense legal document. It is the "ticket" to the closing table.

- What it contains: It lists every condition you must meet to get the money.
  * "Borrower must get hazard insurance."
  * "Borrower must assign a life insurance policy of $1.5M to Lender."
  * "Borrower must provide zoning letter."
- Review it: You should read this carefully. If the SBA requires a $1 million life insurance policy on you, and you

have high blood pressure and cannot get insured, the loan will not close. You need to address this condition now.

## VII. The Closing Gauntlet

Getting the Terms and Conditions sheet is not the end; it is the beginning of the Closing phase. This is where deals often stall.

**1. Life Insurance Delays**

SBA lenders almost always require life insurance on the key owner (you) for the amount of the loan to protect the government if you die.

- *The Trap:* Getting a medical exam and underwriting for a $2 million policy takes 4 to 6 weeks.
- *The Fix:* Apply for life insurance the day you sign the LOI. Do not wait for loan approval. You can always cancel the application if the loan is denied.

**2. The Zoning Letter**

The lender needs a letter from the city/county stating that the property can legally operate as a hotel.

- *The Trap:* Small town zoning offices move at their own pace. If the motel was built in 1960, it might be "legal non-conforming" (grandfathered). Getting the city to put that in writing can take weeks.
- *The Fix:* Ask the seller for their existing zoning compliance letter early, or hire a zoning expeditor now.

**3. Insurance Binders**

You must provide proof of Hazard Insurance (Real Estate), Liability Insurance, and Workers' Compensation.

- *The Trap:* The lender will have specific clauses about the "Mortgagee Clause." If your insurance agent gets one word wrong, the lender's legal counsel will reject the binder.
- *The Fix:* Put your insurance agent in direct contact with the bank's closer.

**4. Equity Injection Audit**

Before the bank releases a dime, they will audit your bank account one last time. They need to see that the $195,000 down payment has left your account and landed in the closing attorney's escrow account. They will match the wire transfer amount exactly to the authorization.

## VIII. Summary Checklist for the Borrower

To manage this process effectively, organize your life into these checklists.

**Raj's Checklist (Acquisition of Independent Motel):**

☐ Financials: 3 years seller tax returns + Interim P&L + Signed 4506-C.

☐ Management Plan: A detailed resume and written plan on how you will market and manage the property (critical for first-time buyers).

☐ Equity: Bank statements proving $195,000 is sitting in your account and seasoned for 2 months.

☐ Entity: Formation documents for your new LLC (Articles of Organization, EIN).

☐ Life Insurance: Application submitted for $1.6M term policy now.

☐ Background: If you have any prior arrests, gather court disposition documents now.

- ☐ Budgeting: Set aside cash for the Appraisal ($3k-$5k) and Phase I Environmental ($2k-$3k) which you pay upfront.

**Anil's Checklist (Expansion/Conversion):**

- ☐ Projections: Month-by-month cash flow showing the "lift" from the new Flag, with royalty fees deducted.
- ☐ PIP Bids: Fixed-price quotes from contractors for the renovation (not back-of-napkin estimates).
- ☐ Franchise Info: Copy of the FDD and the unsigned Franchise Agreement; confirm brand is on SBA Directory.
- ☐ Global Cash Flow: Current debt schedules for your other two hotels.
- ☐ Refinancing: If refinancing debt, ensure it is not with the same bank to avoid PLP loss.

The application process is a test of endurance. By understanding that the lender is bound by these specific SBA SOP rules, you can stop fighting the paperwork and start managing the process. Provide exactly what is asked for, provide it quickly, and keep your eye on the Terms and Conditions sheet. That document is the bridge between your application and your keys.

CHAPTER 5

# DOCUMENTS YOU'LL NEED COMPLETE HOTEL CHECKLIST

Imagine this scenario: your loan officer calls asking for 'just a few more documents.' You scramble through filing cabinets. Three weeks later, they ask for the same documents in a different format. Here's the secret that organized borrowers know: preparation is everything. This chapter ensures that nightmare never happens to you.

## I. Introduction to the Hotel Loan Package

You have found the property. You have negotiated a price. You can see the potential in the lobby and the revenue in the reservation system. Now you face the most significant hurdle in the entire acquisition process: the paperwork.

For a standard small business loan—for a retail store or a landscaping company—the documentation list is long. For a hotel, that list is exponential. You are not buying a business. You are buying a piece of commercial real estate, a complex operational machine, a brand relationship (if franchised), and a heavy inventory of physical assets ranging from shuttle vans to thousands of pillowcases.

SBA lenders view hotels as "special purpose properties." This designation means the building has limited use outside of being a hotel. You cannot easily turn a 40-room motel into a dentist's office without gutting the entire structure. Because the collateral is so specific, the scrutiny is higher. The lender needs to know that the *business* inside the walls can support the debt because the walls themselves are risky collateral.

This chapter provides a comprehensive guide to every document you need to gather. We will use our two examples to illustrate the differences in complexity:

- Raj: A first-time buyer purchasing a 40-room independent highway motel for $1.8 million. He is injecting $180,000 (10%).
- Anil: An experienced operator buying a 55-room underperforming motel and converting it to a Choice Hotels flag. His total project is $2.5 million, including a $600,000 Property Improvement Plan (PIP).

The goal here is to help you assemble a file so complete that the underwriter has no reason to say "no" and no reason to ask for "one more thing" three weeks in a row.

## The SBA Lifecycle: When Do You Need These?

Understanding *when* documents are needed is as important as knowing *what* they are. The process generally follows four stages:

- Pre-Qualification: You provide the "big picture" documents (Tax returns, PFS, STR reports). The lender issues a Term Sheet.
- Underwriting: You provide the detailed operational and legal documents (Entity docs, detailed P&Ls, management agreements). The lender issues a Commitment Letter.
- Closing: You provide the "hard" verifications (Insurance binders, equity injection proof, executed franchise agreements).

- Post-Closing: You provide operational proofs (Liquor license transfer, final renovation receipts).

If you wait until the Closing stage to find your insurance policies or equity proof, you will miss your closing date. Start gathering everything in this chapter the moment you sign the Letter of Intent.

## II. The Core Transaction Documents

Before analyzing operational data, we must establish the legal basis of the deal. These documents prove that you have a valid agreement to purchase the property and that the terms meet SBA requirements.

### A. The Purchase and Sale Agreement (PSA)

The PSA is the constitution of your deal. Lenders read this document line-by-line. In the hotel world, a standard residential real estate contract will not suffice. You need a commercial contract that specifically addresses the three components of a hotel sale.

#### 1. Allocation of Purchase Price

The SBA requires a clear breakdown of what you are buying. Your PSA must allocate the price into three buckets:

- Real Property: The land and the buildings.
- Personal Property (FF&E): Furniture, Fixtures, and Equipment (beds, TVs, laundry machines).
- Intangible Assets (Goodwill): The business name, customer lists, phone numbers, and website domain.

**Why This Matters:** The appraiser will assign a value to these three buckets separately. If your PSA lumps everything into one number without explanation, the appraisal might come back with a different allocation. This can ruin your loan-to-value (LTV) ratios.

**Raj's Scenario:**
Raj submits a PSA for $1.8 million. The contract simply says "Purchase Price: $1.8M." The lender rejects this now. They need to know how much of that is for the land versus the assets. Raj must go back to the seller and add an addendum allocating $1.4M to Real Estate, $300K to FF&E, and $100K to Goodwill.

**2. Required Contingencies**
Your PSA must protect you from specific hotel risks.

- Franchise Contingency: For Anil, this is mandatory. The clause must state that if the franchisor (Choice Hotels) does not approve Anil, or if the Property Improvement Plan (PIP) exceeds a certain dollar amount (e.g., $700,000), Anil can walk away with his deposit.
- Financing Contingency: Never sign a hotel PSA without a clause allowing you to exit if you cannot secure SBA financing.
- Due Diligence Period: Hotels require 30 to 60 days for environmental checks and PIP inspections.

**PSA Checklist for Hotels:**

- ☐ Clear allocation of purchase price (Real Estate vs. Assets vs. Goodwill).
- ☐ Complete inventory list attached as an exhibit.
- ☐ Non-compete agreement terms (e.g., Seller cannot open a hotel within 10 miles for 5 years).
- ☐ Training period terms (how long the seller will stay to train you).
- ☐ Franchise transfer or termination contingencies.
- ☐ Environmental inspection rights (Phase I ESA).

## B. The Letter of Intent (LOI)

While the PSA is the final contract, lenders often ask for the LOI during the pre-qualification stage. This helps them structure the deal before you spend money on attorneys. It shows the "meeting of the minds" about price and terms.

### C. Escrow and Earnest Money Proof

You cannot say you put money down. You must prove it. The SBA requires a paper trail for every dollar used in the transaction.

- Copy of the Cancelled Check: Front and back.
- Bank Statement: Showing the money leaving your account.
- Escrow Letter: A letter from the title company or attorney confirming they are holding the funds.

**Reality Check:** If you paid the deposit in cash or via a "friend," you have created a difficult problem. SBA rules strictly prohibit undocumented cash injections. Everything must be traceable to your personal bank account.

## III. The SBA Application Forms (Government Paperwork)

This section covers the specific federal forms you must complete. These forms are deceptive. They look simple, but incorrect answers here can trigger an automatic decline or a "screen-out" where your file is sent back to the bottom of the pile.

### A. SBA Form 1919: Borrower Information Form

This is the main application form. Every owner with 20% or more equity must sign it.

**Section I: Applicant Information**

- Structure: If you are using an EPC/OC structure (see Chapter 3), you need two sets of Form 1919. One for the Eligible Passive Company (EPC) and one for the Operating Company (OC). Both entities are Co-Borrowers.

- Employees: You must list "Current Employees" and "Jobs Created/Retained."

* *The Trap:* Do not count independent contractors (1099 workers). If your housekeeping staff is outsourced to a third-party agency, they are not employees. Only list W-2 staff.

* *Jobs Retained:* This is usually the current roster of the hotel you are buying.

* *Jobs Created:* Be realistic. If Anil is adding a bar, he might add 2 bartenders. Do not project 50 new jobs for a 55-room motel.

**Section II: Purpose of the Loan**

You must break down exactly how the money will be used. The totals here must match your PSA and your renovation budget.

- Buy Land/Building: $X
- Buy Equipment: $Y
- Renovations: $Z
- Working Capital: $W

**Section III: Legal & Character Questions**

This section asks about criminal history and citizenship.

- Citizenship (Updated March 1, 2026): You must verify status. Only U.S. Citizens and U.S. Nationals with Principal Residence in the United States are eligible. Lawful Permanent Residents (Green Card holders) are no longer eligible to own any percentage of an SBA-financed business under PN 5000-876441.
- Character: If you have any past arrests (even from college 20 years ago), you must disclose them. An arrest does not automatically disqualify you, but *lying* about it does.

## B. SBA Form 413: Personal Financial Statement

This document tells the SBA if you are personally solvent. It must be dated within 90 days of your application submission.

**1. Assets vs. Liabilities**

You must list everything you own and everything you owe.

- Real Estate: Do not guess the value of your home. Use a conservative estimate or a recent tax assessment. If you inflate the value to look rich, the underwriter will question your credibility.
- Retirement Accounts: List your 401(k) and IRAs. While the SBA generally does not require you to liquidate these for the loan, they show your financial strength (reserves).

**2. Contingent Liabilities**

This is the section most borrowers mess up. A "contingent liability" is a debt you *might* have to pay.

- Anil's Scenario: Anil owns two other hotels. He has guaranteed the loans on those properties. He *must* list those loan amounts here as contingent liabilities. Even though the hotels pay the debt, Anil is on the hook if they fail.
- The Co-Signer Trap: If you co-signed a car loan for your child, list it here.

**Why This Matters:** The lender calculates your "Global Cash Flow." They look at your income from all sources and your debt payments from all sources. If you hide a debt and the credit report finds it, the deal is in jeopardy.

## IV. Hotel-Specific Operational Data

This area distinguishes hotel loans from other business loans. You are selling "nights," which is highly perishable inventory. Lenders rely on specific industry reports to verify that your revenue projections are real.

## A. STR Reports (formerly STR, now owned by CoStar Group since 2019)

The STR report is the industry standard for hotel performance data. It compares the subject property against a "Competitive Set" (Comp Set)—usually 5 to 6 nearby hotels of similar class.

**What Lenders Look For:**

- Occupancy Rate: Percentage of rooms sold.
- ADR (Average Daily Rate): The average price paid per room.
- RevPAR (Revenue Per Available Room): Occupancy multiplied by ADR. This is the gold standard metric.
- RevPAR Index (RGI): How the hotel performs relative to the market. An index of 100 means it is performing exactly at the market average. An index of 80 means it is underperforming. An index of 120 means it is outperforming.

**Raj's Scenario (The Independent):**

Raj is buying a "mom and pop" motel. The seller might say, "We don't subscribe to STR." This is a problem. Without third-party data, the lender relies entirely on the seller's tax returns, which may show low income to minimize taxes.

- *The Fix:* Raj should insist the seller buy a "Historical Trend Report" from STR for the past 36 months. If the seller refuses, Raj should pay for it himself ($500-$1,000).
- *The Analysis:* Raj wants to see that the motel's occupancy tracks with the local economy. If the nearby Days Inn and Motel 6 are running at 70% occupancy but his

target motel is at 40%, the lender will ask why. Is it management? Or is the building falling apart?

**Anil's Scenario (The Conversion):**
Anil is buying an underperforming independent motel to turn it into a Choice Hotels property. His STR report likely shows a RevPAR Index of 60% (terrible).

- *The Strategy:* Anil uses this poor report to justify his business plan. He argues: "The market runs at $90 ADR. This hotel runs at $50. By investing $600K and flagging it, I can push the rate to $85." He needs the STR report to prove the *market capacity* exists.

**What You Must Submit:**
☐ Monthly Historical STR Report (past 12-36 months).
☐ Competitive Set definition (list of hotels included in the comparison).
☐ Segmentation Report (optional but helpful: shows weekend vs. weekday, transient vs. group business).

## B. Financial Statements and Tax Verification

You need to provide the history of the business and the history of yourself.

### 1. The 4506-C Process (IRS Verification)

You will sign IRS Form 4506-C. This authorizes the lender to get a transcript of tax returns directly from the IRS.

- The Deal Killer: Lenders compare the tax returns the seller gave you against the transcript from the IRS. If the seller gave you a return showing $100,000 profit, but the IRS transcript shows a loss of $50,000, the deal is dead now due to fraud.

- Requirement: You need transcripts for the seller's business for the last 3 years.

**2. Interim Financials**

Tax returns are historical. Lenders need to know what happened *this year*. You must submit:

- Year-to-Date (YTD) P&L: Dated within 90 days of closing.
- YTD Balance Sheet: Shows current debt and assets.
- Aging Reports: Accounts Receivable and Accounts Payable.

**3. Trailing 12-Month (TTM) P&L**

Hotel revenue is seasonal. A P&L from January to June might look terrible for a beach hotel but great for a ski lodge. Lenders require a TTM P&L. This takes the last 12 months of operations (e.g., August 2023 to August 2024) to smooth out seasonality.

**Raj's Pitfall:** The seller of the independent motel shows a net loss on tax returns but claims, "I make $100,000 in cash that I don't report."

- Lender Reality: If it is not on the tax return, it does not exist. The lender will calculate the Debt Service Coverage Ratio (DSCR) based on the *reported* income. Raj cannot use "add-backs" for unreported cash.

## V. Franchise Documents: The "Directory" Update

For Anil, and anyone buying a branded hotel (Marriott, Hilton, IHG, Choice, Wyndham), this section is the critical path. In the past, lenders had to review every page of the Franchise Agreement. Now, the SBA uses a centralized system.

## A. The SBA Franchise Directory

The lender confirms your brand is listed on the SBA Franchise Directory.

- The Rule: If your brand is on this list, the lender does not need to review the Franchise Agreement for eligibility. They need to check the code.
- The Process: You or your lender will look up "Choice Hotels" or "Hilton" on the SBA website.
- The Code: You will find a "Franchise Identifier Code" (e.g., S1234). This code goes on your application.

**What if the brand is NOT on the Directory?**

If Anil wants to flag his hotel with a new, small brand that is not on the list, the lender cannot approve the loan yet. The franchisor must submit their documents to the SBA Franchise Team for review. This can take weeks. *Pro Tip:* Check the directory before you sign the PSA.

## B. The SBA Addendum (Form 2462)

Most major hotel brands have negotiated a "Standard Addendum" with the SBA.

- What it is: A document signed by the Franchisor and You (the Franchisee). It overrides any part of the Franchise Agreement that conflicts with SBA rules (like forced transfer of assets).
- Requirement: You must provide the *executed* addendum before closing.

## C. The Franchise Agreement and FDD

Even though the Directory streamlines eligibility, you still need to provide the full documents.

- Franchise Disclosure Document (FDD): You must provide the "Receipt of FDD" page, signed and dated. This proves you received the disclosures as required by law.
- Franchise Agreement: The signed contract detailing your royalty fees (e.g., 5% of revenue) and marketing fees. The lender needs these numbers to calculate your monthly cash flow.

## VI. Renovation and Construction (The PIP)

When a franchised hotel changes hands, the brand usually requires a renovation to bring it up to current standards. This is the Property Improvement Plan (PIP).

### A. The PIP Checklist for Anil

- The PIP Inspection Report: Provided by the brand. It lists tasks: "Replace carpet in 55 rooms," "Install 50-inch TVs," "Repave parking lot."
- Cost Estimates/Bids: The brand lists tasks, not prices. Anil must get contractor bids for every line item.

* *Example:* The PIP says "Renovate Lobby." Anil needs a bid from a general contractor for $40,000 detailing the drywall, flooring, and front desk work.

- Timeline: When will the work be done? The SBA usually gives you up to 12 months (sometimes longer for massive projects) to complete the work after closing.

### B. The 15% Contingency Rule

If your renovation is extensive (common in hotel conversions or 504 loans), the SBA has strict rules about cost overruns.

- The New Rule: For major renovations or 504 projects, the SBA requires a 15% contingency fund added to the construction budget.

- Anil's Math: If his contractor bids total $600,000, the loan budget must include an extra $90,000 (15%). This money is set aside. If he doesn't use it, it pays down the principal. If he needs it for surprise plumbing issues, it is there.

### C. "Do-It-Yourself" Restrictions

Anil might think, "I can paint the rooms myself and save money."

- SBA Rule: You can be your own contractor *only* if you are a professional contractor with a license. Even then, you cannot charge a profit—only labor and materials.
- Documentation: You must provide two independent bids for the work to prove your "self-work" cost is reasonable. Most lenders prefer you hire a third-party General Contractor to avoid headaches.

## VII. Management & Corporate Structure

Who is running the show? The SBA has a strict rule: You must be active. Passive investment is not allowed.

### A. The "Passive" Trap and Meaningful Oversight

If you hire a third-party management company (which Anil might do since he has multiple properties), you must be careful. If the management agreement gives the company total control—hiring, firing, check signing, budgeting—without your input, the SBA views you as a "passive investor." The loan will be denied.

**The Fix: Meaningful Oversight**

Your management agreement must explicitly state that you (the owner) retain these four rights:

- Budget Approval: You approve the annual operating budget.

- Capital Expenditures: You approve major repairs or purchases (e.g., over $5,000).
- Bank Accounts: You control the operating accounts.
- Employee Oversight: You have the final say on hiring/firing the General Manager.

**Anil's Strategy:** Anil hires "Keystone Management Company." He submits the contract. The lender's legal team flags a clause saying "Manager has sole discretion over all personnel." Anil's attorney must change this to "Manager directs personnel, subject to Owner's oversight and policy."

### B. Entity Documents (EPC/OC Structure)

Hotels often use a dual structure to separate liability.

- Eligible Passive Company (EPC): The entity that owns the real estate (see Chapter 3 for full explanation).
- Operating Company (OC): An LLC that owns the business, pays the employees, and holds the franchise license.
- Lease Agreement: The EPC leases the building to the OC. The rent payment usually equals the mortgage payment plus a buffer.

**Why This Matters:** Both entities are borrowers. You need documents for *both*:

- Articles of Organization.
- Operating Agreement (listing all owners).
- EIN Letter (Tax ID).

## VIII. Equity and Financial Injection

This is where you prove you can afford the loan. You cannot bring a suitcase of cash to closing.

## A. Proof of Injection (The Cash)

SBA loans generally require 10% to 15% down.

- Raj: Buying for $1.8M. Needs $180,000 (10%).
- Anil: Project is $2.5M. Needs $375,000 (15% due to renovation risk).

**The Paper Trail:**

- Two Months of Bank Statements: Showing the funds in your account.
- Sourcing: If a large deposit ($50,000) appeared one month ago, you must explain it. "I sold a car" requires a bill of sale. "I sold stock" requires a brokerage statement.
- Gift Letter: If Raj's parents give him $50,000, they must sign a standard SBA Gift Letter stating, "This is a gift, not a loan. No repayment is expected."

## B. Standby Debt: The "Secret" Equity

Raj only has $100,000 cash. He needs $180,000. He is short $80,000.

- The Solution: The Seller agrees to "carry a note" for $80,000.
- The Rule: The SBA allows seller debt to count as equity *if* it is on Full Standby.

* Full Standby: This means Raj makes *no payments* (principal or interest) to the seller for the life of the SBA loan (usually 25 years) or until the SBA loan is refinanced.

* The Document: You need a Promissory Note and a Standby Creditor Agreement signed by the seller.

- Benefit: Raj closes the deal with less cash. The seller gets their price (eventually) and interest accrues.

## IX. Debt Refinancing Documents

If Anil is refinancing an existing hotel loan to get better terms or funds for renovation, the documentation burden increases.

**What You Must Submit (Source: SOP 50 10 8):**

- Copy of the Note: The original loan document you are paying off.
- Payment Transcript: Evidence that you have been current on payments for the last 12 months. Any late payment must be explained in detail.
- Release of Lien: Evidence that the old lender will release the collateral upon payment.
- Credit Available Elsewhere Statement: You must prove you cannot get these terms from a conventional bank without the SBA guarantee.

## X. Property and Compliance Due Diligence

This section covers the physical and regulatory checks.

### A. Environmental Reports (Phase I ESA)

Hotels are considered "high risk" for environmental issues. Old laundry facilities may have used harsh chemicals. Maintenance sheds may have spilled oil.

**Requirement:** A Phase I Environmental Site Assessment. An engineer walks the property and checks historical records.

- Clean: Good to go.
- REC (Recognized Environmental Condition): A problem was found. This triggers a Phase II, where they drill into the soil to test samples. This costs $10,000+ and takes weeks.

**Raj's Nightmare:** His Phase I shows the motel was built on top of an old heating oil tank from the 1950s. He cannot close until a Phase II proves the tank isn't leaking.

### B. Insurance

Hotels carry specific risks. You need a binder (proof of coverage) before closing.

- Hazard/Property Insurance: Covers replacement cost of the building.
- General Liability: Slip and falls, food poisoning.
- Liquor Liability: Mandatory if you have a bar.
- Flood Insurance: Mandatory if in a FEMA flood zone.
- Builder's Risk: Mandatory for Anil during his renovation.

**Life Insurance Requirement:**

The lender may require you to get a life insurance policy on yourself.

- When Required: If the value of the collateral (Hotel + Assets) is less than the loan amount (common in business acquisitions with high goodwill).
- The Document: A "Collateral Assignment of Life Insurance" form. This assigns the payout to the lender if you die, paying off the loan.

### C. Licenses

You must prove you can legally run the hotel.

- Business License: Standard city/county permit.
- Liquor License: This is the hardest one. Transferring a liquor license can take months. The lender will often close the loan with a condition that you provide the license within 90 days, or they may require an escrow of funds until the transfer is complete.

## XI. Summary Checklist for Raj and Anil

Here is how the document stack differs for our two buyers.

| Document Category | Raj (Independent, First-Time Buyer) | Anil (Conversion to Flag, Experienced) |
|---|---|---|
| Purchase Agreement | Standard Commercial PSA ($1.8M). | PSA + Franchise Contingency + PIP Cap. |
| Franchise Docs | Not Applicable. | Directory Check, FDD Receipt, Addendum, Franchise Agreement. |
| Renovation/ PIP | Property Condition Report (PCR) only. | PIP Inspection, Contractor Bids, 15% Contingency, Builder's Risk. |
| Operational Data | Historical STR Reports (36 months). | Historical STR + Pro Forma STR (projecting post-reno rates). |
| Management | Resume (must prove transferrable skills). | Management Contract (must pass "Meaningful Oversight" test). |
| Equity Proof | Bank Statements ($100K) + Seller Standby Note ($80K). | Bank Statements ($375K) + Contingent Liability Schedule. |
| Entity Structure | Likely Single LLC (or EPC/OC). | EPC/OC Structure (Real Estate Co. + Operating Co.). |
| Refinancing | N/A (purchase). | Copy of Notes + Payment Transcripts (if refinancing existing debt). |

## XII. Why Deals Fail (The "Screen-Outs")

The SBA Loan Guaranty Processing Center (LGPC) screens files. If documents are missing, they "screen out" the file. This means they stop working on it and send it back to the bottom of the pile.

**Common Screen-Out Reasons for Hotels:**

1. Missing Franchise Addendum: The lender submits the file hoping the franchisor will sign it later. SBA says "No."
2. Incomplete Equity Verification: A bank statement shows a large deposit, but there is no paper trail explaining it.
3. Passive Management Agreement: The management contract gives away too much control to the operator.
4. Expired Financials: The P&L is 120 days old. It must be within 90 days.
5. Allocations Mismatch: The Appraisal says the Real Estate is worth $1M, but the PSA says it is worth $1.5M.
6. Tax Transcript Mismatch: The 4506-C return from the IRS does not match the tax return provided by the seller.

## XIII. Action Plan: How to Organize This Chaos

1. Create a Digital Data Room: Use Dropbox, Google Drive, or a secure portal. Do not email documents one by one.
2. Folder Structure: Create folders matching the sections above (Legal, Financial, Property, Franchise, Equity).
3. Naming Convention: Name files clearly. "2023_Tax_Return_Final.pdf" is better than "Scan0043.pdf."
4. The "Request List": Ask your lender for their specific closing checklist now. Do not wait for them to drip-feed requests to you.

Getting a hotel loan is a marathon. The documentation is the terrain. If you map it out early, verify your STRs, secure your franchise docs, and clean up your financials, you will cross the finish line while other buyers are still arguing over a missing bank statement.

For Raj, the focus is on proving the *past* performance justifies the price. For Anil, the focus is on proving the *future* performance justifies the renovation. Both require a mountain of paper, but now you know exactly what that mountain looks like.

CHAPTER 6

# WHAT LENDERS LOOK FOR HOW HOTELS GET EVALUATED

Here's the truth that most hotel buyers learn too late: the lender doesn't see your property the way you do. You see potential. They see risk. You see a renovation opportunity. They see a special-purpose asset that's hard to liquidate. Understanding how lenders evaluate hotels is the secret to getting approved.

Lenders view hotels fundamentally differently than they view office buildings, retail centers, or warehouses. If an office building owner goes bankrupt, the bank can evict them and lease the space to a law firm or an insurance broker. The walls and roof have inherent value independent of the tenant.

A hotel is different. The value of the building is tied directly to the business operation within it. If the business fails, the building is a collection of bedrooms with no kitchen, likely zoned only for transient lodging. It cannot easily be converted into apartments or offices without massive capital.

This chapter explains exactly how SBA lenders evaluate hospitality deals. We will look at the specific metrics they calculate, the rigorous stress tests they apply to your projections, and the regulatory hurdles found in SBA Standard Operating Procedure (SOP) 50 10 8 that apply specifically to the lodging industry.

To make this concrete, we will follow two applicants through the review process:

- Raj: A first-time buyer acquiring a 40-room independent motel on a highway for $1.8 million. He has $180,000 (10%) for his equity injection.
- Anil: An experienced operator with two existing properties. He is buying a 55-room unbranded motel and converting it to a Choice Hotels flag. His total project cost is $2.5 million, which includes a $600,000 Property Improvement Plan (PIP).

## I. The Structure: EPC and OC

Before we discuss revenue or occupancy, we must address the legal structure of the deal. If you get this wrong, your loan is ineligible regardless of how profitable the hotel is.

In almost every SBA hotel loan, the lender requires you to split your business into two separate entities.

- Eligible Passive Company (EPC): The real estate holding entity (see Chapter 3).
- Operating Company (OC): This entity owns the business operations. It hires the staff, holds the franchise license, pays the bills, and collects the room revenue.

### Why This Structure Exists

Lenders and savvy borrowers prefer this structure for liability protection. If a guest slips in the shower and sues the hotel, they are suing the Operating Company. The real estate (held by the EPC) remains shielded from that specific lawsuit in many jurisdictions.

However, the SBA has strict rules about this arrangement (Source 49).

### The Lease Requirement

There must be a formal lease agreement between your EPC and your OC.

- Term: The term of the lease must use a duration at least equal to the term of the loan. If you get a 25-year SBA loan, the lease between your two companies must be for at least 25 years (or fewer years with renewable options that equal 25 years).
- Rent: The rent paid by the OC to the EPC must be enough to cover the loan payments.
- Guaranties: Both entities are on the hook. The EPC is the borrower (because it owns the collateral), and the OC must be a co-borrower or a guarantor. This means the SBA looks at the financials of *both* entities combined.

**The Raj Scenario:**

Raj initially set up a single LLC to own the building and run the motel.

- Lender Feedback: The lender advises him to split it. Raj forms "Raj Motel Holdings, LLC" (EPC) for the building and "Raj Hospitality Services, LLC" (OC) for the operations.
- The Pitfall: Raj forgets to draft the lease before closing. The lender cannot close the loan without the executed lease in the file. This delays his closing by two weeks while his attorney drafts a document that is essentially Raj renting the building to himself.

## II. Affiliation and Size Standards

SBA loans are for "small" businesses. But in the hotel world, "small" is defined generously.

According to the SBA Size Standards (Source 50), a hotel (NAICS 721110) is considered small if its average annual receipts are under $40 million. This is a massive number. You can own a profitable full-service hotel and still qualify.

## The Affiliation Trap

The complexity arises when you own multiple hotels. The SBA views "affiliation" through ownership and control (Source 77). If you own 51% of Hotel A and 51% of Hotel B, the SBA considers them affiliates. To determine if you are "small," the SBA adds the revenue of Hotel A and Hotel B together.

**The Anil Scenario:**

Anil already owns two hotels.

- Hotel 1 Revenue: $12 million
- Hotel 2 Revenue: $15 million
- Target Hotel Revenue: $4 million

Total Revenue: $31 million. Anil is still under the $40 million cap, so he is eligible.

However, consider if Anil had a partner. Let's say Anil's wealthy brother-in-law, Vikram, owns 10 hotels with $80 million in revenue. Vikram wants to invest in Anil's new deal and take a 51% share.

- The Problem: Because Vikram controls the new company (51%), the SBA deems the new company affiliated with Vikram's 10 other hotels.
- The Result: The aggregate revenue is $80 million + $31 million = $111 million. This exceeds the $40 million cap. The loan is ineligible.

**Pro Tip:** If you have wealthy investors who own other large businesses, keep their ownership share under 50% to avoid "affiliation by ownership" issues, provided they do not also control the management.

## III. The "Big Three" Performance Metrics

When you purchase a manufacturing business, lenders look at EBITDA (Earnings Before Interest, Taxes, Depreciation, and Amortization). When you purchase a hotel, lenders look at the "Big Three" industry metrics first. These figures form the foundation of the pro forma income statements required for your loan application.

You must understand these numbers better than your lender does. If you cannot explain why your ADR is trailing the competitive set, you will struggle to get funded.

### A. Occupancy Rate

This is the percentage of available rooms sold during a specific period. It measures demand.

**The Formula:**
Total Rooms Sold / Total Rooms Available

**How Lenders Evaluate It:**
Lenders do not look at occupancy in a vacuum. They compare the subject property's historical occupancy against the "competitive set" (local competitors). This data usually comes from a STR Report (STR), which is the industry norm for benchmarking.

Many lenders also check online reviews. A quick look at online reviews, Google Reviews, or Booking.com ratings tells a story that financial statements cannot. A hotel with a 2.5-star average and complaints about cleanliness, rude staff, or noisy rooms raises underwriting concerns. Lenders know reviews can be manipulated (both inflated and sabotaged by competitors), so they look for patterns than person complaints. If you are buying a property with poor reviews, address this proactively. Explain what caused the problems and how you plan to fix them. Be transparent; lenders appreciate honesty about challenges more than they appreciate borrowers who pretend problems do not exist.

**The Raj Scenario:**
Raj is buying a 40-room independent motel. The historical occupancy is 45%. The average occupancy for economy motels in his highway corridor is 60%.

- Lender's View: This is a red flag. Why is this property underperforming the market by 15 points? Is it dirty? Is it invisible on Expedia? Is the signage broken?
- The Fix: Raj cannot say "I'll fix it." He needs to provide a corrective action plan. "The previous owner did not list on Booking.com. I have already drafted the listing. The signage is unlit; my budget includes $15,000 for a new LED pole sign."

### B. Average Daily Rate (ADR)

This is the average rental income per paid occupied room. It measures pricing power.

**The Formula:**
Room Revenue / Number of Rooms Sold

**How Lenders Evaluate It:**
Lenders assess if the ADR is sustainable based on the property condition and the local economy. They worry about "race to the bottom" pricing wars. If your only strategy to fill rooms is to drop the price to $49/night, your profit margins will vanish because the cost to clean the room (labor, laundry, supplies) remains the same regardless of the room rate.

**The Anil Scenario:**
Anil is converting a generic motel to a Choice Hotels flag. The current ADR is $65. He projects the ADR will jump to $95 after the renovation and branding.

- Lender Verification: The lender will not take Anil's word for it. They will pull data on other Choice properties in similar markets. If other branded hotels in the area are getting $100+, Anil's projection of $95 is credible. If they are getting $75, his loan application will be denied for unrealistic projections.

### C. RevPAR (Revenue Per Available Room)

This is the primary industry metric. It combines demand (occupancy) and price (ADR) into a single figure about the property's ability to make money.

**The Formula:**
Occupancy Rate × ADR

*OR*

Total Room Revenue / Total Available Rooms

**Why This Matters:**
You can have 100% occupancy by selling rooms for $1. You can have a $500 ADR by selling one room a year. Neither makes money. RevPAR balances them.

**Lender's Analysis:**
Lenders use RevPAR to determine the "Repayment Ability." They track the RevPAR Index (or Revenue Generation Index - RGI).

- RGI = 100: You are performing exactly inline with the market.
- RGI > 100: You are outperforming the market.

- RGI < 100: You are underperforming.

If you are buying a property with an RGI of 80 (underperforming), you must explain the *operational* reason why. If you cannot identify the problem, the lender assumes the problem is the location or the building itself, neither of which you can fix easily.

## IV. The Stress Test: DSCR and Cash Flow

Once the lender accepts your revenue assumptions (Occupancy and ADR), they move to the bottom line. The SBA has strict rules on cash flow coverage.

### A. Debt Service Coverage Ratio (DSCR)

The SBA minimum DSCR is **1:1** (Source 22, Source 65). This means for every $1.00 of loan payment, the business must generate $1.00 in cash flow.

Reality Check: While the SBA allows 1:1, few lenders will approve a loan with zero margin for error. Most lenders require a minimum DSCR of 1.15 to 1.25. They want to see that you have a 15% to 25% cushion to absorb a bad month or an unexpected repair (like a boiler blowing up in January).

**The Calculation:**

(Net Operating Income + Depreciation + Amortization + Interest + One-time Expenses) / (Total Annual Loan Payments + Interest)

Legitimate addbacks can improve your DSCR calculation. If the seller paid themselves $150,000 when the market rate for a general manager is $75,000, lenders may allow you to add back the $75,000 excess as "owner compensation above market." Similarly, if family members are on payroll at above-market rates, that excess can be added back. However, you must be prepared to justify market rates. Bring comparable salary data from industry sources like STR or hotel management associations. If you claim the GM position should pay $75,000, be ready to prove it. Lenders are skeptical of aggressive addbacks that conveniently make marginal deals work.

**The Raj Scenario:**

- Loan Request: $1.62 million ($1.8M price minus $180K equity).
- Interest Rate: Prime + 2.75%. Let's assume 11% total for this example.
- Amortization: 25 years (standard for real estate).
- Annual Payment: $190,000.
- Required Cash Flow (at 1.25x): $237,500.

If the motel's tax returns from last year show a Net Operating Income (NOI) of only $150,000, Raj has a problem. He is short by nearly $90,000.

**The "Add-Back" Negotiation:**

Raj can argue for "add-backs" to normalize the cash flow.

- *Allowable Add-Backs:* The seller's personal car lease, a one-time repair (like a new roof paid in cash), or salary paid to a family member who wasn't working.
- *Disallowed Add-Backs:* "Potential" revenue from improvements not yet made, or underestimating utility costs.

Because Raj is a first-time buyer, lenders will likely discount his projected operational improvements. They will rely heavily on the **historical** tax returns of the seller (Source 9). If the historicals don't support the loan, Raj might be declined unless he puts more money down to lower the loan amount.

## B. Global Cash Flow Analysis

For experienced operators, lenders analyze the "Global Cash Flow" of the borrower and their affiliates (Source 7). This is where Anil has a significant advantage.

**The Anil Scenario:**
Anil's new project involves a renovation (PIP). During the 6-month renovation, the hotel might be closed or running at partial capacity. The DSCR on the *new* hotel might be 0.5:1 (losing money) during construction.

However, Anil owns two other hotels.

- Hotel A: Generates $200k surplus cash flow.
- Hotel B: Generates $150k surplus cash flow.

The lender combines the cash flow of the new project, the two existing hotels, and Anil's personal debt/income. If the *combined* entity meets the 1.15:1 Global DSCR requirement, the loan can be approved (Source 10). The existing hotels effectively subsidize the new one during its ramp-up period.

## C. The Lender's Stress Test

Lenders do not accept your numbers. They break them. They will run a sensitivity analysis to see how fragile your business model is.

**Sample Stress Test Table:**

| Metric | Base Case (Your Projection) | Stress Case 1 (Market Dip) | Stress Case 2 (Recession) |
|---|---|---|---|
| Occupancy | 65% | 60% | 55% |
| ADR | $100 | $95 | $90 |
| Revenue | $2,372,500 | $2,080,500 | $1,806,750 |
| NOI | $830,000 | $650,000 | $480,000 |
| Debt Service | $600,000 | $600,000 | $600,000 |
| DSCR | 1.38x (Pass) | 1.08x (Pass/Weak) | 0.80x (Fail) |

If a 10% drop in occupancy causes your loan to default (Stress Case 2), the lender considers the deal "thin." They may ask for a higher down payment (equity injection) to reduce the debt service and improve the ratio.

## V. Valuation and Appraisal: The "Going Concern"

Valuing a hotel is complex because you are valuing three things at once:

- Real Estate: The land and bricks.
- FF&E: Furniture, Fixtures, and Equipment (beds, TVs, laundry machines).
- Intangible Assets: Goodwill, business value, and the franchise flag.

### A. The Special Appraiser Requirement

You cannot use a residential appraiser or even a general commercial appraiser who usually values warehouses.

Because the hotel is a "Special Purpose Property," the SBA requires the appraiser to be a Certified General Real Property Appraiser. Also, if the "Going Concern" value (the business value) is used to justify the loan, the appraiser must have completed at least four similar going concern appraisals within the last 36 months (Source 18).

**Why This Matters:** Finding an appraiser with these specific credentials in a rural area can be difficult. It often costs more ($4,000 - $7,000) and takes longer (4 to 6 weeks) than a standard appraisal. Plan your closing timeline accordingly.

### B. Allocation of Value

The appraisal will break down the value.

- Real Estate: $1,200,000
- FF&E: $300,000
- Intangible/Business Value: $300,000
- Total: $1,800,000

**The Blue Sky Trap:**

If the Intangible Value ("Blue Sky") is too high, lenders get nervous. Real estate stays put. Furniture can be sold. But "Goodwill" evaporates instantly if the operator runs the business poorly. If the appraisal comes back with 50% of the value in "Intangibles," the lender may reduce the loan amount because the hard collateral is insufficient.

### C. "As-Completed" Value

For projects involving substantial renovation, like Anil's PIP, the appraisal is ordered on an **"As-Completed"** basis (Source 17).

The appraiser assumes the renovations are finished and the hotel is flagged.

- Current Value: $1.9 Million
- Renovation Cost: $600,000
- As-Completed Value: $3.2 Million

In this scenario, Anil has created $700,000 in equity by doing the work ($3.2M Value - $2.5M Cost). Lenders love this because it improves the Loan-to-Value (LTV) ratio now upon completion.

## VI. Managing the PIP: Draws and Construction

If you are buying a franchised hotel, you will almost certainly have a Property Improvement Plan (PIP). This is a list of renovations required by the brand (Choice, Wyndham, Marriott) to grant the license.

Lenders treat the PIP as a mini-construction loan. This process confuses many first-time borrowers.

### The Money is Controlled

The lender does not give Anil a check for $600,000 at closing. The money is placed in a "controlled account" or escrow.

## The Draw Process

Anil must front the costs or get the work done, then ask for reimbursement.

- Step 1: The contractor installs the new carpet and sends an invoice for $50,000.
- Step 2: Anil submits a "Draw Request" to the lender with the invoice.
- Step 3: The lender sends a third-party inspector (often an architect or engineer) to the hotel to verify the carpet is installed (Source 30).
- Step 4: The lender collects "Lien Waivers" from the contractor. This is a legal document where the contractor promises not to put a lien on the building because they have been paid.
- Step 5: The lender wires the $50,000.

**The Cost:** Every time the inspector comes out, it costs money (usually $500 - $1,000). If Anil requests a draw every week, he will burn through his budget in inspection fees. It is better to bundle the work and do 4 or 5 large draws.

## The Contingency Fund

Lenders universally require a contingency fund, usually 10% of the construction budget (Source 30/17). If Anil's PIP is $600,000, the budget will be $660,000.

- Why: Construction always goes over budget. You open a wall and find mold. You rip up carpet and find cracked concrete.
- Who Pays: You do. The contingency is usually part of the loan, but if you exceed it, you must pay the difference from your own pocket.

## VII. Operational Flags vs. Independent

The decision to flag (franchise) or stay independent drastically alters the risk profile and the underwriting requirements.

### A. Flagged Hotels (Franchise)

Lenders generally prefer flags. A Hampton Inn or a Holiday Inn Express comes with a national reservation system, a loyalty program (points), and standardized quality. It removes the "marketing risk."

**The Requirements:**

- Franchise Agreement: The lender must review the Franchise Disclosure Document (FDD).
- Comfort Letter: This is a non-negotiable legal document between the lender and the franchisor. It allows the lender to take over the franchise license if they have to foreclose on you. Without this, the lender's collateral is a building, not a branded business.
- Royalty Impact: Lenders will deduct franchise fees (royalties usually 8-12% of gross revenue) from the NOI. Anil needs to show that the increase in ADR and Occupancy from the flag outweighs the 10% royalty cost.

### B. Independent Hotels

Independent hotels offer higher margins (no royalties) and freedom. But they have higher "Key Person" risk.

**The Requirements:**

Lenders will scrutinize your marketing plan. How will you fill rooms? If you rely solely on drive-by traffic, you are vulnerable to a new bypass road or a competitor with a better billboard.

**The Raj Scenario:**
Raj avoids franchise fees, which improves his bottom line. However, he is a first-time buyer with an unbranded property.

- The Stress Test: The lender will likely stress-test his revenue harder. "What if occupancy drops 10%? You don't have a loyalty program to fall back on."
- The Equity Consequence: Because the risk is higher, the lender might ask for *more* than the minimum 10% equity, or require a larger post-closing liquidity reserve.

## VIII. Equity Injection: Skin in the Game

How much money do you need?

### A. Minimum Injection

For a complete change of ownership, the SBA requires a minimum equity injection of **10% of total project costs** (Source 6).

**The Raj Scenario:**
Raj is buying for $1.8M. He *must* inject at least $180,000.

### B. Seller Financing Rules

Can the seller help? Yes, but with strict limits.

- Partial Standby: If the seller carries a note and you make payments on it now, that debt is treated like a bank loan. It counts against your DSCR, but it does *not* count as equity.
- Full Standby: If the seller carries a note and agrees to take no payments (principal or interest) for the life of the SBA loan (Source 6), that debt can count toward your equity injection.
- The Half-and-Half Rule: Seller debt on full standby can only satisfy *half* the required equity. Raj needs 10%

($180k). The seller can carry $90k on standby, but Raj *must* bring the other $90k in cash.

### C. Borrowed Equity

You generally cannot borrow your down payment. The SBA wants to see your own cash at risk. However, there is an exception: You can borrow the money if you have an outside source of repayment (Source 6).

- *Example:* Raj takes a Home Equity Line of Credit (HELOC) on his house. He can use this for the injection *if* his salary from his IT job is enough to pay the HELOC payments. The hotel cash flow cannot be used to pay the HELOC.

## IX. Specialized Insurance and Zoning Risks

Hotels carry specific risks that trigger specific insurance requirements.

### A. Life Insurance

The SBA requires life insurance on the "Key Person" for the business (Source 56).

- Requirement: If Raj dies, the hotel operation might collapse. The lender will require an assignment of a life insurance policy on Raj's life for the amount of the loan (or at least the unguaranteed portion).
- Timing: This is the number one cause of closing delays. Getting a medical exam and underwriting for life insurance takes weeks. Start this process the day you sign the term sheet.

### B. Ordinance and Law Insurance

Many older motels are "Legal Non-Conforming" uses.

- *Scenario:* Raj's motel was built in 1970. It is set back 10 feet from the road. The current city zoning code requires a 30-foot setback.
- *The Risk:* If the motel burns down (more than 50% damage), the city might enforce the new code. Raj would have to rebuild 30 feet back, which might make the building smaller or impossible to build.
- *The Fix:* Lenders require Ordinance and Law insurance coverage. This pays for the demolition of the undamaged portion of the building and the increased cost of construction to meet new codes.

### C. Zoning Verification

Before closing, the lender will require a Zoning Letter from the municipality stating that the hotel is a legal use and, importantly, whether it can be rebuilt if destroyed. If the city says "No rebuild allowed," the loan is dead.

## X. Environmental Pitfalls

Hotels are often located on prime commercial corners. Unfortunately, those corners were often gas stations in the 1950s.

### The Phase I ESA

Lenders almost always require a Phase I Environmental Site Assessment (Source 7, Appendix 7). An environmental engineer inspects the history of the land.

**The Dry Cleaner Trap:**

Full-service hotels often had on-site dry cleaning plants in the past. Dry cleaning chemicals (PERC) sink into the foundation and soil.

- If the Phase I shows a "Recognized Environmental Condition" (REC) related to an old dry cleaner or a nearby gas station, the lender will require a Phase II.
- A Phase II involves drilling into the soil to test samples. It costs $10,000+ and takes weeks.
- If contamination is found, the deal usually dies unless the seller agrees to remediate it (which is expensive).

## Summary: From Application to Approval

To move from "Risky Special Purpose Property" to "Approved Loan," you must present a cohesive story supported by data.

**For Raj (The First-Timer):**

- Focus: Structure the EPC/OC correctly now. Hire a professional General Manager to solve the "experience" gap. Have a detailed marketing plan to fix the occupancy issue. Ensure the Life Insurance application is started early.

**For Anil (The Developer):**

- Focus: Ensure the "Affiliation" rules don't push him over the size standard. Build a 10% contingency into the PIP budget. Prepare the Global Cash Flow analysis to show how existing hotels will support the renovation period.

When you speak the language of RevPAR, PIP Draws, Global DSCR, and Comfort Letters, you show to the lender that you are not a dreamer with a vision of a painted lobby. You are an operator who understands the mechanics of the hospitality business. That confidence is what gets the loan approved.

CHAPTER 7

# COLLATERAL AND PERSONAL GUARANTEES

Nobody tells you this before you start: the collateral conversation is where dreams meet reality. You've found the property, passed eligibility, chosen your program, survived the application—and now the lender wants to know what you're putting on the line. This chapter shows you exactly what to expect.

When a lender hands you a term sheet, they are essentially asking two questions. First, "Can this business generate enough cash to pay us back?" This is the Debt Service Coverage Ratio (DSCR), which we discussed in previous chapters. Second, and equally important, is the question we will answer here: "What happens if it doesn't?"

This section covers collateral and personal guarantees.

For many borrowers, this is the most emotional part of the process. It involves letting a stranger appraise the value of your life's work. It involves signing documents that pledge your personal assets—potentially even your home—to the bank. It involves uncomfortable conversations about life insurance and spousal liability.

However, fear comes from the unknown. Once you understand the mechanics of how the SBA and lenders view collateral, you can manage this process with confidence. Let us examine how these rules affect Raj and Anil differently.

**Raj is borrowing $1.62 million for his $1.8 million motel acquisition. With only a 10% equity injection ($180,000), he is "all in" on this deal—which affects how lenders view his collateral position.**

**Anil's $2.5 million project involves more complexity. He has significant assets from his two existing hotels, but also a portfolio of LLCs that creates collateral considerations we will explore.**

In this chapter, we will break down exactly what the lender requires from both of them, why they require it, and how you can prepare.

## I. Real Estate as Collateral

Real estate is the gold standard of collateral for SBA lenders. Unlike inventory that can spoil, or equipment that becomes obsolete, land and buildings generally hold value. Consequently, the valuation of the real estate you are buying (or renovating) is the anchor of your loan structure.

### Commercial Real Estate Appraisal Requirements

You might think the property is worth $1.8 million because that is what you are paying for it. The lender does not agree. The lender believes the property is worth whatever a disinterested third-party appraiser says it is worth.

The SBA has strict rules derived from the Uniform Standards of Professional Appraisal Practice (USPAP). The most significant distinction lies in who performs the appraisal.

State-Certified vs. State-Licensed

The SBA distinguishes between appraisers based on the transaction size.

- Transactions under $1,000,000: A State-licensed appraiser is acceptable.
- Transactions over $1,000,000: The appraiser must be State-certified.

**Why This Matters:**
State-certified appraisers are more experienced and charge higher fees. More importantly, there are fewer of them. In rural areas or during busy market cycles, finding a State-certified appraiser can take weeks.

**Reality Check:** You cannot hire the appraiser. Even though you pay for the report, the lender must engage the appraiser directly to ensure independence. If the seller hands you an appraisal from six months ago, toss it. The lender cannot use it.

**Scenario: Raj's Appraisal**
Raj is buying his motel for $1.8 million. Because this is above the $1 million threshold, his lender must hire a State-certified appraiser. Raj tries to save money by asking if they can use a "restricted use" report or a broker's price opinion (BPO). The answer is a hard no. The lender must order a full self-contained appraisal report.

## "As-Is" vs. "As-Completed" Valuations

The type of value the appraiser estimates depends entirely on whether you are buying the keys or if you are picking up a hammer.

"As-Is" Valuation

For a straightforward acquisition where you continue operations as they are, the appraiser provides an "As-Is" market value. They look at the historical financials of the business, the condition of the building today, and comparable sales in the area.

"As-Completed" Valuation (Renovations)

If the loan finances substantial renovation, the lender needs to know what the property *will* be worth once you finish the work. "Substantial" is defined by the SBA as rehabilitation expenses exceeding one-third of the purchase price or fair market value.

**Scenario: Anil's Renovation**

Anil is buying a run-down property for $1.9 million. He is investing $600,000 into a PIP to flag it as a Choice Hotel.

- $600,000 is about 31% of the purchase price.
- Even though this is technically under the "substantial" threshold of one-third, the lender will likely still demand an "As-Completed" or "As-Stabilized" appraisal.
- Why? Because Anil is banking on the "Choice Hotels" flag to drive revenue. The appraiser needs to validate that a flagged hotel in that specific location is worth $2.5 million (Anil's total cost).

If the appraiser says the hotel, even with the renovation and the flag, is only worth $2.2 million, Anil has a problem. He is $300,000 underwater on paper before he even opens the doors.

## Special Purpose Properties

Some properties are designed for a specific use and are difficult to convert to other uses. These are known as Special Purpose Properties. Common examples include hotels, gas stations, car washes, and nursing homes.

If you are buying a Special Purpose Property, the appraisal rules are stricter. The appraiser must be a Certified General Real Property Appraiser and must allocate the value between:

- Land
- Improvements (Building)
- Equipment (FF&E)
- Business Value (Intangibles/Goodwill)

**Why This Matters:**

A standard commercial appraiser who usually values office buildings might not know how to value a hotel correctly. They might value the bricks and mortar, ignoring the income generated by the business. This results in a low appraisal. You must ensure your lender hires an appraiser with specific experience in your industry (e.g., hospitality or petroleum).

## The EPC/OC Structure

If you are buying real estate for your business, you will likely encounter the **Eligible Passive Company (EPC)** and **Operating Company (OC)** structure. This is a requirement for most SBA real estate deals to protect your assets.

**How it Works:**

- EPC (Eligible Passive Company): The real estate holding entity described in Chapter 3.
- OC (Operating Company): This is your main business entity. It employs the staff, sells the goods, and runs the daily operations.
- The Lease: The EPC leases the building to the OC. The OC pays rent to the EPC. The EPC uses that rent to pay the SBA loan.

**Anil's Structure:**

Anil sets up "Anil Real Estate LLC" (EPC) to purchase the hotel and "Anil Hotel Operations LLC" (OC) to run it.

**The Rules You Must Follow:**

- The Lease Term: The lease between your EPC and OC must have a remaining term at least equal to the term of the loan. If you have a 25-year SBA loan, you need a 25-year lease (or a shorter lease with renewable options totaling 25 years).
- Rent Limitation: The rent the OC pays the EPC cannot be arbitrary. It serves as a flow-through. The rent generally equals the debt service payment plus a reasonable allowance for holding costs (taxes, insurance, maintenance).

Anil cannot charge his OC double the market rent to move profits into his real estate company.

- Co-Borrowers: Both the EPC and the OC must be co-borrowers or guarantors on the loan. Both are liable.

## II. Environmental Investigations: The Hidden Deal Killer

Before a bank takes a building as collateral, they need to know what is in the ground underneath it. If the soil is contaminated, the property value could be zero—or worse, it could be a liability. The SBA has rigorous environmental policies.

### Level 1: RSRA (Records Search with Risk Assessment)

For "low risk" properties (like a standard office condo or a retail store in a strip mall), the lender starts with an RSRA. This is a database search of government records to see if there are known contamination sites nearby.

- Cost: Low ($300–$600).
- Time: Fast (3–5 days).
- Outcome: If the RSRA comes back "Low Risk," you are done.

### Level 2: Phase I Environmental Site Assessment (ESA)

For properties with higher risk factors, an RSRA is not enough. You must pay for a Phase I ESA. This involves an environmental engineer visiting the site, interviewing owners, and reviewing historical records going back decades.

**Mandatory Phase I Triggers:**

- Dry Cleaners (current or past).
- Gas Stations.
- Auto Repair Shops.

- Motels/Hotels: This often catches buyers like Raj. If the motel was built before 1980, or if it has an on-site commercial laundry facility that historically used strong solvents, a Phase I is usually required.

**Scenario: Raj's Laundry Problem**

Raj's motel has been operating since 1965. The RSRA shows a dry cleaner operated across the street in the 1980s. Because of the age of the property and the proximity to a high-risk facility, the lender requires a Phase I ESA.

- Cost: $2,000–$3,000.
- Time: 3–4 weeks.
- Result: If the engineer finds "Recognized Environmental Conditions" (RECs), you cannot close yet.

### Level 3: Phase II (Testing)

If the Phase I identifies a REC (e.g., "There was a gas station here in 1950 and we don't have records of tank removal"), you must move to Phase II. This involves drilling into the soil and testing groundwater.

- Cost: Expensive ($5,000–$20,000+).
- Time: Slow (4–8 weeks).

**Deal Killer Alert:** If contamination is found, the deal often dies. The SBA *can* approve loans on contaminated property, but only if the issue is remediated or if there is a strong indemnification agreement from the seller or a state fund. Most sellers refuse to indemnify, and most buyers walk away.

## III. The Collateral Shortfall and "Fully Secured" Rule

This is where the math gets serious. The SBA wants loans to be "fully secured" whenever possible. This means the **Liquidation Value** of the collateral should equal or exceed the loan amount.

**Note:** We use Liquidation Value, not Market Value.

- Commercial Real Estate: Typically discounted to 85% of market value.
- Residential Real Estate: Typically discounted to 80% of market value.
- Equipment: Typically discounted to 50% (used) or 75% (new).

## Calculating the Gap

If the liquidation value of your business assets is lower than the loan amount, you have a **Collateral Shortfall**.

**Scenario: Raj's Gap**

Raj is borrowing $1.62 million.

- Appraised Market Value: $1.8 million.
- Lender's Liquidation Value (85%): $1.53 million.
- Math: $1.62M Loan - $1.53M Collateral = $90,000 Shortfall.
- Consequence: Because the loan is not fully secured by the business assets, the lender must look at Raj's personal assets to bridge the gap.

**Scenario: Anil's Portfolio**

Anil has a shortfall on the new project because of construction risk. However, Anil owns two other motels.

- Motel A: Worth $3M, owed $1M. (Huge equity).
- Motel B: Worth $2M, owed $1.8M. (Little equity).
- The lender may require Anil to grant a Junior Lien (a second mortgage) on Motel A. Because there is significant equity there, this more collateral might "fully secure" the new loan, potentially saving Anil from having to pledge his personal residence.

### Fighting a Low Appraisal (The Rebuttal)

What if the appraisal comes in lower than the purchase price? This creates a massive shortfall and usually violates the Loan-to-Value (LTV) requirements.

**You have three options:**

- Renegotiate: Show the appraisal to the seller. "The bank says it's only worth $1.6M. I can't pay $1.8M."
- Cash to Close: If the seller won't budge, you must pay the difference in cash. The bank will not lend on the portion of the price that exceeds the value.
- The Appraisal Rebuttal: If you believe the appraiser made a factual error, you can submit a formal rebuttal.

* How to do it: Do not say "It's worth more." You must find specific errors. Did they use the wrong square footage? Did they compare your renovated hotel to a teardown motel 20 miles away? Did they ignore a recent revenue spike?

* Process: Submit your data to the lender. The lender submits it to the appraiser. The appraiser decides whether to adjust the value. (Success rate is low, but not zero).

## IV. Personal Real Estate (The House)

This is the rule that catches most borrowers off guard and causes the most friction at the dinner table.

The Rule: If the loan is not fully secured by business assets (which, as we saw with Raj, happens often), the lender generally must take a lien on the personal residence of any owner with 20% or more ownership *if there is equity in the home.*

## The 25% Equity Exception

There is a specific calculation lenders use to determine if they *must* take your house.

**The 25% Rule:** The lender does not have to lien your primary residence if the equity in the home is less than 25% of the Fair Market Value.

**Let's run the numbers:**

- Home Value: $600,000.
- Existing Mortgage: $500,000.
- Equity: $100,000.
- Calculation: $100,000 is only 16.6% of $600,000.
- Result: Since 16.6% is less than 25%, the SBA does not mandate a lien. The lender *could* still ask for it (out of an abundance of caution), but you have grounds to argue against it.

**Contrast this with Raj:**

- Home Value: $500,000.
- Existing Mortgage: $300,000.
- Equity: $200,000.
- Calculation: $200,000 is 40% of the value.
- Result: The lender must take a lien on Raj's house up to the amount of the collateral shortfall ($90,000).

## Homestead Laws vs. Federal Law

If you are in a state like Texas or Florida often say, "You can't lien my house; I have Homestead protection."

The Reality: Federal law supersedes state law. When you sign an SBA loan document, you are effectively waiving your Homestead protection about the lien placement. The lender *can* put the lien on the house.

However, the SBA generally respects state laws about forced foreclosure. This means that while the lien sits on your house, they likely cannot kick you out and sell the house to pay the debt (unless you sell the house voluntarily or refinance, at which point the lien must be paid). The lien acts as a "cloud on title" ensuring that if you ever realize the value of the home, the SBA gets paid.

Useful Step: Documents to Gather Now

If you suspect you have a collateral shortfall, gather these documents about your home now to prevent closing delays:

- Mortgage Statement: Most recent, showing current balance.
- Homeowners Insurance: Declaration page.
- Title Policy: From when you bought the house.
- Value Estimate: A Zillow printout or tax assessment is usually enough for the first file, though the bank will order a formal limited appraisal or BPO later.

## V. Business Personal Property (FF&E)

Hotels, restaurants, and medical practices are heavy on Furniture, Fixtures, and Equipment (FF&E). In a hotel, this includes beds, televisions, lobby furniture, commercial laundry machines, and kitchen equipment.

### Valuation: Net Book Value vs. Appraisal

There are two ways to value these assets: **Net Book Value (NBV)** or **Appraisal**.

Net Book Value (The Depreciation Problem)

Net Book Value is the original cost of the item minus accumulated depreciation. For tax purposes, businesses aggressively depreciate assets to lower their tax bills (using Section 179 expensing).

**Scenario: The "Worthless" Furniture**
Raj is buying the motel. The seller provides a list of furniture and claims it is worth $200,000. Raj agrees; the furniture looks decent.

However, the seller has owned the motel for 10 years. On the seller's tax return, he has fully depreciated that furniture. The Net Book Value is effectively zero.

**The Problem:** If the lender uses Net Book Value, they assign $0 collateral value to the furniture. This increases Raj's collateral shortfall, making it a certainty they will lien his house.

Independent Equipment Appraisal

If Raj wants the bank to give him credit for the $200,000 worth of furniture, he must order an **independent equipment appraisal**.

- The Rule: If the valuation of fixed assets is greater than their Net Book Value, an independent appraisal is mandatory.
- Discount Rates: Even with an appraisal, the bank does not give you 100 cents on the dollar.

* New Equipment: Typically discounted to 75% of invoice/cost.

* Used Equipment: Typically discounted to 50% of Net Book Value or 80% of Orderly Liquidation Value (OLV).

**Anil's Strategy:**
Anil is buying $200,000 of *new* furniture for his Choice Hotels renovation. Because he has invoices proving the cost of new goods, the lender can use 75% of that invoice amount ($150,000) as collateral value without needing a separate appraisal.

## The PMSI Conflict

Often, businesses lease specific equipment than buying it. For example, Anil might lease the 55 televisions for his new rooms from a vendor. The vendor will file a Purchase Money Security Interest

(PMSI). This gives the vendor the right to repossess the TVs if Anil stops paying.

**The Conflict:** The SBA lender wants a "first lien" on all business assets. The TV vendor also wants a "first lien" on the TVs.

**The Solution:** This is standard. The SBA lender will allow the PMSI, but they may require an Intercreditor Agreement or simply carve out the TVs from their collateral list. Be sure to disclose all equipment leases early to avoid last-minute legal hurdles.

### Landlord Waivers (For Leased Locations)

If you are buying a business that leases its space (like a restaurant in a strip mall, or if Anil's OC leases from his EPC), you need a **Landlord Waiver**.

**The Issue:** If you don't pay your rent, the landlord has the legal right to lock you out and seize your equipment (the "Landlord's Lien"). If you don't pay your SBA loan, the bank wants to seize that same equipment.

**The Document:** The Landlord Waiver is an agreement where the landlord:

- Subordinates their lien rights to the bank.
- Grants the bank the right to enter the premises to inspect or liquidate the equipment (usually for a period of 30–60 days).

**Strategy:** Landlords hate signing these. They often feel it infringes on their rights.

- Pro Tip: Introduce this requirement early. Do not wait until three days before closing.
- The Script: Tell your landlord: "My lender requires a standard access agreement so they can finance my

improvements. It doesn't change your lease terms; it lets them pick up their equipment if I go out of business."

## VI. Intangible Assets and Goodwill

When you purchase a business, you are usually paying more than the value of the land and the old furniture. You are paying for cash flow, the brand, the customer list, and the "Blue Sky." Accountants call this Goodwill.

SBA loans can finance Goodwill, but the value must be proven.

**The $250,000 Threshold:**

For a Change of Ownership transaction, if the amount you are financing (minus the appraised value of real estate and equipment) exceeds **$250,000**, you must get an independent business valuation from a "Qualified Source."

**What is a Qualified Source?**

- Certified Business Appraiser (CBA)
- Accredited Senior Appraiser (ASA)
- Certified Public Accountant (CPA) who performs valuations (ABV)

**Scenario: Anil's Acquisition**

- Purchase Price: $1.9 million.
- Real Estate Appraised Value: $1.5 million.
- FF&E Value: $100,000.
- Implied Goodwill: $300,000.

Because the goodwill ($300,000) is over the $250,000 threshold, Anil cannot agree on the price with the seller. The appraiser must certify that the business operations justify that extra $300,000. If the valuation comes back showing only $100,000 in goodwill, the bank will cut the loan amount, and Anil will have to bring an extra $200,000 in cash to close the deal.

Pro Tip for Buyers: Make your purchase contract contingent on the business valuation and appraisal. If the numbers don't match the price, you need an "out" or a mechanism to renegotiate.

## VII. Personal Guarantee Requirements

The SBA guarantee protects the bank. The Personal Guarantee protects the SBA.

When you sign a personal guarantee, you are promising that if the business fails and the liquidation of assets doesn't cover the debt, you will pay the difference from your personal funds. This liability is "unlimited."

### The 20% Rule

The Mandate: Any person or entity that owns 20% or more of the applicant business must provide an unlimited full personal guaranty (SBA Form 148).

#### Scenario: Raj's Ownership

Raj owns 100% of the acquiring entity. He signs the full guarantee. There is no way around this.

#### Scenario: Partnership Structure

Imagine Raj brings in two partners.

- Raj: 60%
- Partner B: 30%
- Partner C: 10%

**Who signs?**

- Raj (60%): Yes.
- Partner B (30%): Yes.
- Partner C (10%): No. (Technically not required by SBA, but the *lender* can still ask for it if Partner C is a key manager).

## Spousal Guarantees

This is often a source of tension in loan closings. You might ask: "My spouse has nothing to do with the business. Why do they have to sign?"

There are two main reasons a spouse signs, and they are different:

- Combined Ownership (The 20% Loophole Closer):

If a spouse owns less than 20%, but the *combined* ownership of both spouses equals or exceeds 20%, the spouse must guarantee the loan.

* *Example:* Raj owns 15%. His wife owns 5%. Neither hits the 20% mark individually. But combined, they own 20%. Therefore, both must provide full personal guarantees.

1. Perfection of Lien (The Non-Owner Spouse):

If the spouse owns 0% of the business, but the lender is taking a lien on the couple's jointly owned home, the spouse must sign documents.

*Important Distinction:* In this case, the spouse usually signs a Limited Guaranty (Form 148L). This document specifically limits their liability to their interest in the collateral (the house). They are not pledging their salary, their separate bank accounts, or their retirement funds. They are simply acknowledging that the house is on the line. Understanding this distinction is vital for explaining the requirement to a skeptical spouse.

**Reality Check:** If you live in a Community Property state (like California, Texas, Arizona), the rules are stricter. Lenders almost always require spousal signatures to legally access the assets of the community estate.

### Corporate Guarantees

Anil's situation is more complex. He owns his other two motels in separate LLCs (Motel A LLC and Motel B LLC).

- Does Motel A LLC guarantee the loan for the new motel?

Usually, no. The SBA looks for person human guarantors. However, if Anil is using equity from Motel A to secure the new loan (via a Junior Lien), Motel A LLC will be a Corporate Guarantor.

- Does Anil guarantee it?

Yes. Regardless of how many LLC layers he creates, Anil (the human) is the beneficial owner. He cannot hide behind a corporate veil for an SBA loan.

## VIII. Insurance Requirements

You probably expect to purchase hazard insurance. Few expect the laundry list of other policies the lender will demand.

### Life Insurance

This requirement has evolved. Historically, the SBA required life insurance for every loan. Now, per SOP 50 10 8, the SBA defers to the lender's internal policy for most standard loans.

**However, Life Insurance IS required if:**

- The business is a Sole Proprietorship or Single Member LLC.
- The business is legally dependent on the active participation of one owner.
- There is a Collateral Shortfall.

**Scenario: Raj's Requirement**

Raj has a $90,000 collateral shortfall and he is the sole operator. If he dies, the motel likely fails. The lender will view him as a "Key Person" and require a policy assignment.

- Amount: Usually equal to the loan amount or the shortfall amount.
- Mechanism: You must execute a Collateral Assignment. This is a legal document filed with the insurer stating that if you die, the bank gets paid first (up to the loan balance). Your family gets the rest.
- Pro Tip: Term life insurance is cheap and acceptable. You can pledge an existing policy; you don't always need a new one.

## Hazard and Flood Insurance

**Real Estate:**
The SBA requires **Replacement Cost** coverage. This is different from "Actual Cash Value" (ACV). If your building burns down, ACV pays you what the old building was worth (depreciated). Replacement Cost pays you what it costs to build a new one. The bank demands the latter.

**Flood Insurance:**
If your property is in a Special Flood Hazard Area (SFHA) according to FEMA maps, flood insurance is mandatory.

- No Exceptions: Even if "it never floods here," if the map says Zone A or V, you must buy the insurance.
- Personal Property: If the building is in a flood zone, your equipment inside must also be insured against flood.

### Liability and Dram Shop

- General Liability: Standard slip-and-fall coverage.
- Dram Shop (Liquor Liability): If you are buying a hotel with a bar, or a restaurant that serves alcohol, this is mandatory. It protects against lawsuits if a patron gets drunk at your establishment and causes an accident.

## IX. Advanced Scenarios: Construction and Renovations

For borrowers like Anil, the collateral picture changes during the life of the loan. This is known as construction risk.

### The "Risk of Failure"

If Anil runs out of money halfway through the $600,000 renovation, the bank is holding collateral that is worth *less* than when they started (a gutted building is worth less than an operating motel).

To mitigate this, lenders use strict controls:

- Fund Control: The bank does not give Anil the $600,000. They hold it in escrow. Anil submits invoices from contractors. The bank inspects the work. Then the bank pays the contractor directly.
- Lien Waivers: Before releasing a payment, the bank requires the contractor to sign a waiver stating they have been paid for the work to date and surrender their right to file a mechanic's lien on the property.

**Mechanic's Liens:**

If a contractor is not paid, they can file a lien on the property that supersedes the bank's mortgage in some states. Banks want to avoid this risk. Anil needs to warn his contractor that "SBA draws take time." If the contractor walks off the job because payment takes 10 days instead of 2, the project halts.

## X. Checklist: Collateral and Guarantee Documents

When you are approaching closing, your inbox will flood with requests. Use this checklist to stay organized.

### Real Estate Documents

- ☐ Appraisal Report: Ordered by the lender, compliant with USPAP.
- ☐ Phase I Environmental: Or RSRA for low-risk properties.
- ☐ Title Insurance Commitment: Ensures no prior liens exist.
- ☐ Survey: Confirms property lines and easements.
- ☐ Flood Hazard Determination: Confirms if flood insurance is needed.
- ☐ Landlord Waiver: If the business premises are leased.

### Personal Property & Business Assets

- ☐ UCC-1 Search: Ensures the seller hasn't already pledged the equipment.
- ☐ Equipment List: Detailed inventory with serial numbers.
- ☐ Equipment Appraisal: If asking for value above Net Book Value.

### Guarantees & Legal

- ☐ SBA Form 148: Unconditional Guarantee for all 20%+ owners.
- ☐ SBA Form 148L: Limited Guarantee for non-owner spouses (if applicable).
- ☐ Trust Certification: If assets are held in a family trust.
- ☐ Operating Agreement: For the EPC and OC entities.

### Insurance

- ☐ Hazard Insurance: Replacement cost coverage. Lender listed as "Mortgagee."
- ☐ General Liability Insurance: Standard business coverage.
- ☐ Life Insurance Policy: With Collateral Assignment.
- ☐ Flood Insurance: (If in Zone A/V).
- ☐ Dram Shop Liability: (If alcohol is served).

## XI. Closing Thoughts on Risk

It is natural to resent the lender for these requirements. It feels invasive to have your house liened, your life insured, and your soil tested.

However, try to reframe this perspective. The lender is providing you with high-use capital (often 90% LTV) that conventional banks would never offer. In exchange for taking that outsized risk, they require outsized security.

**Raj's Path:** He accepts the lien on his home as the price of admission for becoming a business owner. He works hard to pay down the loan. In three years, if the property value appreciates and the loan balance drops, he can ask the bank to release the lien on his house. (They might say no, but he can ask).

**Anil's Path:** He uses his portfolio strength to negotiate. He offers a larger equity injection in exchange for keeping his personal residence free and clear. Collateral is the safety net. Your job, through strong operations and cash flow management, is to ensure the bank never has to use it.

In the next chapter, we will discuss the specific closing process and how to get from "Approved" to "Funded" without losing your mind.

CHAPTER 8

# HOW TO USE YOUR LOAN PROCEEDS

The biggest mistake borrowers make after approval is assuming they can spend the money however they want. Here's the truth: SBA loan proceeds come with strict rules. Break them, and you risk your entire loan. This chapter shows you exactly what you can purchase, what you cannot buy, and how to structure your request.

When you apply for a standard mortgage to purchase a house, the bank rarely asks if you plan to purchase new curtains or fix the roof with the leftover cash. They give you the money to purchase the house, and your personal budget is your own business.

SBA lending is entirely different.

The Small Business Administration and your lender care deeply about exactly where every single dollar goes. They care because the federal government guarantees a portion of the loan. This guarantee requires strict adherence to the "Use of Proceeds" rules outlined in the SBA's Standard Operating Procedures (SOP 50 10). If you spend the money on the wrong thing, you jeopardize the guarantee. If the guarantee is jeopardized, the lender loses their safety net. Consequently, lenders police the flow of funds with extreme rigor.

This chapter breaks down exactly what you can purchase, what

you cannot buy, and how to structure your request so that you get the capital you need without triggering a decline from underwriting. We will move beyond the basics and explain the specific documentation lenders require to prove you spent the money correctly.
We will follow two specific scenarios to illustrate these rules:

- Raj: A first-time buyer acquiring a 40-room independent highway motel for $1.8 million. He has $180,000 for his equity injection.

## I. The Sources and Uses Equation

The "Sources and Uses" statement is the central nervous system of your loan application. This document tells the lender two things. First, it tells them where the money is coming from (the Source), such as the bank loan, your equity injection, or a seller note. Second, it tells them exactly where the money is going (the Use).

These two columns must balance to the penny.

If you ask for a $2 million loan but can only justify $1.9 million in eligible expenses, the lender will not write you a check for the difference to keep as "rainy day" money. They will simply reduce the loan amount. SBA loans are invoice-based or receipt-based lending. You generally do not receive lump sums of cash without a specific, documented purpose.

### The "Rainy Day" Fallacy

If this is your first deal, you might assume they should ask for the maximum amount possible "in case." They might say, "I need $1.8 million for the hotel, but let's ask for $2 million so I have a cushion."

The SBA does not allow for a vague "cushion." Every dollar must have a name. If you want a cushion, you must label it "Working Capital," and you must justify why your business needs that specific amount based on cash flow projections. If you cannot prove you need it for operations, you cannot borrow it.

## Verifying the "Sources"

Before we discuss how you spend the money, you must understand how the lender views the money coming in. The "Sources" side usually consists of:

- Bank Loan: The amount the lender provides.
- Equity Injection: The cash you put into the deal.
- Seller Note: Money the seller lends you (often to bridge a gap).

**The Equity Trap:**

You cannot simply show the lender a screenshot of a bank account and say, "Here is my equity." The lender is required by SBA rules to verify the *source* of your equity.

- If it is cash on hand: You need three months of bank statements showing the money was there.
- If it is a gift: You need a gift letter and proof of the donor's ability to give it.
- If it is borrowed: You generally cannot borrow your equity injection unless you have an outside source of income (like a spouse's salary) that can service that new debt independent of the business you are buying.

**Why This Matters:**

If you cannot prove where your equity came from, the lender cannot count it as a "Source." If your Sources decrease, your Uses must decrease, which means you might not have enough money to purchase the hotel.

## II. Acquisition: Buying the Hotel (Real Estate & Business)

The most common use of SBA 7(a) loan proceeds in the hospitality industry is the acquisition of an existing facility. This includes the land, the building, and the business operations. While this seems straightforward, the structure of the buy changes how the loan is processed.

### Change of Ownership: Asset vs. Stock Purchase

When Raj buys the highway motel, he is engaging in a "Change of Ownership." The SBA allows loan proceeds to be used for this, but the legal structure matters.

**1. Asset Purchase**

Almost all small hotel transactions are "Asset Purchases." This means Raj creates a new LLC. That new LLC uses the loan to purchase the assets (building, land, name, customer list) from the Seller's LLC.

- Pros: Raj starts with a clean slate about liability. He does not inherit the seller's potential lawsuits, hidden debts, or unpaid taxes.
- SBA View: This is the preferred method. The SBA considers this a buy of 100% of the assets.

**2. Stock Purchase**

A "Stock Purchase" is where Raj buys the membership interests (or stock) of the Seller's LLC. Instead of buying the building, he buys the company that owns the building.

- The Risk: Raj inherits everything that company ever did. If the previous owner didn't pay overtime to a housekeeper three years ago, Raj is now liable.
- Why Do It? In the hospitality industry, sometimes you must do a stock purchase to preserve a valuable liquor

license or gaming license that cannot be easily transferred to a new entity.

- SBA Requirement: If Raj does a stock purchase, the SBA requires that the business entity he is buying must be a Co-Borrower on the loan. The company itself becomes liable for the debt used to purchase it. This is a strict compliance rule that often surprises sellers.

## The Valuation Cap

This is a rule that breaks many deals. The SBA states that the loan amount for a change of ownership cannot exceed the **business valuation**.

Let us look at Raj's deal.

- Contract Price: $1.8 million.
- Raj's Equity: $180,000 (10%).
- Loan Request: $1.62 million.

The lender will order a business appraisal. If the appraiser says the hotel is only worth $1.7 million, the SBA will strictly limit the financing based on that value. Raj cannot borrow against a purchase price that exceeds the value.

**The Shortfall Rule:**

If the valuation comes in low ($1.7 million) and the seller refuses to lower the price from $1.8 million, Raj has a problem. He can still buy the hotel, but he cannot use the SBA loan to cover the $100,000 gap. He must pay that $100,000 out of his own pocket *in addition* to his required equity injection. The loan proceeds cannot cover the "air" (the overpayment) in the deal.

## Allocating Goodwill vs. Real Estate

When Raj fills out his application, the "Use of Proceeds" section for acquisition will be broken down based on the appraisal.

**Raj's Sources and Uses:**

| Source | Amount | Use | Amount |
|---|---|---|---|
| SBA Loan | $1,620,000 | Land Purchase | $400,000 |
| Equity Injection | $180,000 | Building Purchase | $1,100,000 |
| | | FF&E (Existing) | $200,000 |
| | | Goodwill/Intangibles | $100,000 |
| Total | $1,800,000 | Total | $1,800,000 |

**Why This Matters:**
Lenders hate "Goodwill" (also called Blue Sky). Goodwill is the value of the business reputation above the value of the hard assets. If Raj defaults, the bank can sell the land and building. They cannot easily sell "Goodwill." If the Goodwill portion of the purchase price is too high (usually over $500,000), the lender may require more equity from Raj to mitigate their risk.

## The 51% Occupancy Rule

For hotel buyers, this is critical. To use SBA 7(a) funds to purchase a building, your business must occupy at least 51% of the square footage.

**The Scenario:**
Raj's motel has a large restaurant attached to the lobby. The restaurant space is 3,000 square feet. The motel lobby and back office are 2,000 square feet. The guest rooms are separate.

- If Raj leases the restaurant to a third-party operator (like a Denny's), he might violate the occupancy rule depending on how the square footage is calculated relative to the total "rentable property."
- The Rule: If you are buying an existing building, your Operating Company (the hotel) must occupy 51% of the

space. If you are building a *new* hotel, you must occupy 60% initially.

- Trap: If Raj buys a mixed-use building with a small hotel on top and three large retail stores on the bottom, the SBA might view this as "Passive Income" (investment property) than an operating business. Passive income properties are ineligible for SBA financing.

## III. Renovations and Property Improvement Plans (PIPs)

If you are buying a franchised hotel (like a Holiday Inn Express, Hampton Inn, or Choice Hotel), you will encounter a PIP: Property Improvement Plan. Even independent hotels like Raj's often need renovation. The SBA allows you to include these costs in the loan, which is a massive advantage over conventional bank loans that often refuse to fund future construction.

However, construction is the highest-risk activity for a lender. If the contractor walks off the job, the hotel cannot open, revenue stops, and the loan defaults. Therefore, the rules here are intense.

### The Scenario: Anil's Conversion

Anil is buying a 55-room unbranded motel. He wants to convert it to a Choice Hotels flag. The franchise agreement requires him to complete a $600,000 renovation to bring the property up to brand standards. This includes new signage, new beds, lobby upgrades, and an electronic key card system.

**Total Project:**

- Acquisition Price: $1.9 million.
- PIP/Renovation Budget: $600,000.
- Total Project Cost: $2.5 million.

### Rule 1: Fixed-Price Contracts

You cannot effectively manage a renovation on a "cost-plus" basis with SBA funds. The lender requires a **fixed-price contract** with a general contractor. This contract must detail exactly what work will be done for exactly what price.

- Anil's Action: He cannot tell the bank "I think it will cost $600,000." He needs a signed bid from a contractor breaking down the cost of paint, carpet, and labor.

### Rule 2: The 10% Contingency

Renovations never go exactly to plan. You open a wall and find mold. You rip up carpet and find cracked concrete. The SBA and prudent lenders strongly recommend (and often mandate) a **contingency fund**. This is usually 10% of the construction budget.

- Revised Budget for Anil: $600,000 Renovation + $60,000 Contingency (10%) = $660,000.
- Loan Structure: The lender adds this $60,000 to the loan amount. If Anil does not use it, the principal is reduced. If he needs it, it is there.

### Rule 3: Performance Bonds vs. Fund Control

This is the most common point of friction in hotel renovations.

**The Requirement:**

For construction budgets over $350,000 (like Anil's $600,000 project), the SBA generally requires the contractor to provide a **100% Payment and Performance Bond**.

- What it is: An insurance policy. If the contractor goes bankrupt halfway through the job, the bond company pays to finish the hotel.

- The Problem: Many small, local contractors cannot get these bonds. They are expensive and require audited financials.

**The Workaround: Fund Control**

If Anil's contractor cannot get a bond, the lender can ask the SBA to waive the requirement. In exchange, the lender must use a "Fund Control" or "Voucher Control" system.

- The $600,000 does not go to Anil. It sits in a restricted account.
- The contractor finishes the lobby and submits an invoice.
- The lender sends a third-party inspector to the hotel to verify the work is done and the materials are on-site.
- The inspector signs off.
- The lender (or fund control company) wires the money directly to the contractor.
- Lien Waivers: The contractor must sign a document stating they have been paid and surrender their right to sue the property for that amount.

**Why This Matters:**

Anil must understand he will not have control of the checkbook. He needs to hire a contractor who is willing to wait for bank inspections and draw disbursements. If the contractor demands "50% upfront cash," they are not compatible with SBA lending.

## Rule 4: "Do It Yourself" Restrictions

Anil might think, "I can save money if I act as my own General Contractor."

SBA rules generally prohibit the borrower from paying themselves or their own company for labor unless they are a professional contractor by trade with a proven track record. You cannot pay yourself a "project management fee" from the loan proceeds. The money must go to third-party vendors and material suppliers.

## IV. Furniture, Fixtures, and Equipment (FF&E)

Hotels are nothing without FF&E. Beds, dressers, televisions, lobby chairs, breakfast equipment, and laundry machines are eligible uses of loan proceeds.

## The "Useful Life" Rule

This is a technical rule that can shorten your loan term. The SBA requires that the maturity of the loan (how long you have to pay it back) does not exceed the useful life of the assets being financed.

- Real Estate: 25-year useful life.
- FF&E (Beds/TVs): 10-year useful life.
- Working Capital: 10-year useful life.

If Raj buys a hotel where the real estate is $1.6 million and the equipment is $200,000, the "weighted average" useful life is clearly mostly real estate. The lender can comfortably give him a 25-year term.

However, if you are doing a "leasehold improvement" deal (where you rent the building but buy the equipment) or a loan heavily weighted toward equipment, the lender might be forced to shorten the loan to 10 or 15 years. This significantly increases your monthly payment.

**Pro Tip:** For major acquisitions like Raj's, the SBA allows a "blended" maturity. Because the real estate is the dominant asset, the entire loan (including the FF&E portion) usually gets the full 25-year amortization. This is vital for cash flow.

### FF&E in the Sources and Uses

You must be specific. "Miscellaneous" is not an eligible use of proceeds. You need a list.

- Allowable: 40 King Mattresses ($20,000), 40 LED TVs ($12,000), Commercial Washer/Dryer ($15,000).
- Anil's Strategy: Anil provides the lender with the vendor quotes for the furniture package mandated by Choice Hotels. The lender approves this specific list.

## V. Working Capital

Working capital is the most misunderstood category of loan proceeds. It is also the most vital for survival.

**Definition:** Working capital is financing for everyday operations and short-term operational needs.

### Eligible Working Capital Expenses

- Payroll: You can use proceeds to pay the salary of the front desk clerks, housekeepers, and maintenance staff.
- Inventory: Soap, shampoo, breakfast ingredients, linens, cleaning chemicals.
- Utilities: Deposits for electricity and water, plus the monthly bills.
- Marketing: The cost of the "Grand Opening" banner, website development, or first digital ads.

### The Scenario: Raj's Safety Net

Raj is taking over a motel that has been poorly managed. Occupancy is low (40%). He believes he can get it to 65% in six months, but until then, the revenue might not cover the mortgage and the expenses.

Raj requests **$50,000 in Working Capital** as part of his loan.

- Closing: On the day he buys the hotel, the lender deposits $50,000 into Raj's business checking account.
- Usage: In Month 1, Raj is short $8,000 on cash flow because he hired new staff. He uses the working capital to make payroll. In Month 2, he is short $4,000. By Month 4, he is breaking even.

**Why This Matters:**
Without this allocated working capital, Raj would have to use his personal credit cards or emergency savings to pay employees. If he runs out of personal cash, the business fails.

### Restrictions on Working Capital

- Paying Owners: You generally cannot use working capital proceeds to pay the owner's salary during the startup phase unless it was specifically negotiated and included in the business plan. You absolutely cannot use it to reimburse yourself for your equity injection.
- Paying the Seller: You cannot use working capital to pay the seller for things that should have been in the purchase price. However, SBA rules do allow for Buyer Rebates. If the seller agrees to give money back to the business to help with operations, that is allowed, but it usually reduces the loan amount first.
- Construction: If you allocated $50,000 for working capital, you cannot decide to use it to build a swimming pool. That is a construction expense, not working capital.

## VI. Debt Refinancing

SBA 7(a) loans are excellent tools for refinancing existing high-interest debt, but the eligibility rules are tighter than for acquisitions. You cannot refinance any debt you want.

## The "Current" Rule

The most important rule for refinancing is that the government will not bail out a dying loan. The debt to be refinanced must be "Current."

**The Definition:**

"Current" means the loan has had **no payments more than 29 days late** for the last 12 months (or the life of the loan, if less than 12 months).

- No Exceptions: If Anil missed a payment 4 months ago on the loan he wants to refinance, that loan is ineligible. He cannot use SBA funds to pay it off.
- Verification: The lender will demand a 12-month payment transcript (history) from the bank holding the current debt.

## The "10% Improvement" Rule

This is the math test your refinance request must pass. To justify using government-guaranteed funds to pay off private debt, you must save money.

**The Rule:**

The new installment payment amount must be at least 10 percent less than the existing installment amount(s).

**The Scenario: Anil's Bridge Loan**

Anil has a high-interest "hard money" bridge loan on one of his other properties.

- Current Debt: $500,000 balance. 10% interest. 15-year amortization. Monthly Payment: ~$5,373.

- Proposed SBA Refinance: $500,000 balance. 11.5% interest (SBA rates are currently high). 25-year amortization. Monthly Payment: ~$5,087.

**The Test:**

- Current Payment: $5,373
- Target Payment (10% less): $4,835
- New Payment: $5,087

**Result:** The new payment ($5,087) is *not* 10% lower than the old payment ($5,373). **Fail.** This debt is ineligible for refinancing under the standard rule.

**The Loophole: Balloon Payments**

There is a major exception to the 10% rule. If the existing debt has a **Balloon Payment** coming due, or is a **Demand Note** (where the bank can call the loan at any time), the 10% improvement rule *does not apply*. The SBA recognizes that saving you from a massive balloon payment is a valid business purpose, regardless of the monthly payment savings.

### Refinancing Same Institution Debt (SID)

If you are applying for an SBA loan at Bank A to pay off a non-SBA loan you already have at Bank A, this is called "Refinancing Same Institution Debt."

The SBA watches this closely to ensure Bank A isn't trying to shift the risk of a bad loan onto the taxpayer.

- Conflict of Interest: The lender cannot refinance a loan that is already in trouble. It must be perfectly current.
- Loss Shift: If the bank is in a position to sustain a loss (e.g., the collateral value has dropped), they cannot use the SBA loan to bail themselves out.

### Refinancing Credit Card Debt

Many small business owners run operations on credit cards. You *can* refinance this debt, but it is difficult.

- The Certification Trap: You must certify that *every single charge* on that card was for business.
- The Reality: If there is one charge for Netflix or a family dinner on that Capital One statement, the lender may disqualify the entire balance.
- Documentation: You need statements and a specific certification that the debt was exclusively for business.

## VII. Fees and Closing Costs (The "Silent" Use)

When calculating how much money you need, do not forget the costs of getting the loan itself. These are substantial, but fortunately, they are eligible uses of proceeds.

### The SBA Guaranty Fee

This is the upfront fee paid to SBA for the loan guarantee.

- Cost: 0% for loans up to $1M; tiered 3.5%-3.75% for larger loans (see fee matrix in earlier chapter).
- Example: Raj's $1.62M loan costs $42,500 in guarantee fees.
- Good News: You can roll this fee into the loan amount. You do not have to pay it out of pocket.

### Packaging and Legal Fees

- Lender Packaging Fee: Banks often charge $2,000 to $4,000 to structure the file.
- Legal Fees: Commercial real estate closings require attorneys. Expect $3,000 to $10,000 depending on complexity.

- Third-Party Reports: Appraisal ($3,000+), Environmental Report ($2,000+).

**Pro Tip:**
When building your "Uses" budget, always create a line item for "Closing Costs" totaling 3% of the loan amount. If the actual costs are lower, the lender simply reduces the loan at the end. If you forget to include them, you will have to pay them cash at closing.

## VIII. Ineligible Uses: What You Cannot Buy

The SBA has a list of prohibitions. If your Sources and Uses statement includes these, your loan will be denied.

### Passive Income

SBA loans are for *operating* businesses.

- Eligible: Running a hotel where you provide maid service, front desk, and daily turnover.
- Ineligible: Buying an apartment complex where you sign 12-month leases and collect rent.
- The Trap: If Raj buys a hotel that is primarily a "residential hotel" where guests stay for months and there are no services provided, the SBA may deem it passive and ineligible.

### Payments to Owners (Distributions)

You cannot use loan proceeds to pay dividends, distributions, or "draws" to the owners.

- Reality Check: You cannot borrow $100,000 extra to put back in your personal savings account because "you worked hard on the deal." The equity you put in stays in.

### Delinquent Taxes

SBA proceeds generally cannot be used to pay past-due trust taxes (payroll taxes or sales taxes). These are funds you were supposed to hold in trust for the government. If you spent them, the government will not lend you money to pay them back.

- *Exception:* You might be able to pay delinquent *income* taxes if you have an approved payment plan with the IRS and have been current on that plan for a specific period.

### Relocation

You generally cannot use SBA funds to move your business if it causes a net reduction of jobs in the community you are leaving, or if you are moving simply to avoid labor laws. This is rare for hotels (you can't move a building), but relevant for other businesses.

## IX. Summary Checklist for Borrowers

To ensure your loan gets approved and funded without delay, you must present a clean, balanced, and eligible "Sources and Uses" statement. Use this checklist before submitting your application.

### The "Sources and Uses" Checklist

**1. Acquisition Costs**

☐ Purchase Price matches the Purchase Agreement exactly.

☐ Price allocation (Land/Building/Goodwill) is supported by the appraisal.

☐ Occupancy calculation confirms you occupy at least 51% of the building.

**2. Renovation / PIP (if applicable)**

- ☐ Hard construction bid (Fixed Price) from a licensed contractor.
- ☐ 10% Contingency fund added to the budget.
- ☐ Decision made on Payment/Performance Bond vs. Fund Control waiver.

**3. Equipment / FF&E**

- ☐ Itemized list of furniture and equipment to be purchased.
- ☐ Vendor quotes for major items (PMS system, phone system, signage).

**4. Working Capital**

- ☐ Amount calculated based on projected cash flow deficits (months 1-6).
- ☐ Justification written in the business plan (e.g., "Funds needed for first inventory and marketing launch").

**5. Debt Refinance (if applicable)**

- ☐ Copies of Promissory Notes for all debt to be paid off.
- ☐ 12-month payment transcript showing NO payments >29 days late.
- ☐ Calculation showing 10% reduction in monthly payments (unless it is a balloon note).
- ☐ For Credit Cards: Certification that 100% of charges were business-related.

**6. Closing Costs**

- ☐ SBA Guarantee Fee included (0% for loans up to $1M; tiered 3.5%-3.75% for loans over $1M as of FY 2025).
- ☐ Lender Packaging Fee included.
- ☐ Appraisal and Environmental Report costs included.
- ☐ Title Insurance and Attorney fees included.

## The Balancing Act

Finally, verify that **Total Sources = Total Uses**.

- Sources: Loan + Verified Cash Injection + Seller Note.
- Uses: buy + Renovations + Soft Costs + Closing Costs + Working Capital.

If Anil needs $2.5 million for the project but only has a $1.9 million loan and $250,000 cash, he is short. He cannot close until he finds the missing source.

**Final Pro Tip:** Always round up your cost estimates slightly in the beginning. It is much easier to reduce the loan amount at the end than to ask for more money two weeks before closing.

By strictly adhering to these use-of-proceeds rules, you protect your loan eligibility and ensure a smoother path to the closing table. In the next chapter, we will discuss the Collateral requirements—what assets you have to pledge to secure this money.

CHAPTER 9

# AFTER APPROVAL CLOSING, FUNDING, AND LOAN MANAGEMENT

Picture this moment: after months of applications, appraisals, and negotiations, your lender calls with three words that change everything—'You are approved.' Here's what nobody tells you about what happens next. The celebration is premature. The real work is just beginning.

You received the commitment letter. You signed the term sheet. You popped the champagne.

Now put the cork back in the bottle.

Getting an SBA loan approval is a massive victory, but many borrowers confuse "approval" with "funding." These are two distinct phases of the lending lifecycle. The period between receiving your approval email and seeing the wire hit your bank account is known as the closing process. For many small business owners, this phase is more stressful than the first application.

During the application phase, you were selling your vision. During the closing phase, you are satisfying the regulators. The SBA 7(a) program is a government-guaranteed program. That guarantee is only valid if the lender follows the Standard Operating Procedures

(SOP) with absolute precision. If the lender makes a mistake on the closing paperwork, the government can strip the guarantee. If that happens, the lender loses their insurance policy on your loan.

Because of this dynamic, your lender will suddenly become extremely strict. They will ask for documents you are certain you already sent. They will demand insurance policies with specific wording. They will require signatures from your spouse. They are not doing this to annoy you. They are doing this because a single missing signature can void the government guarantee.

This chapter guides you through the transition from approval to closing, explains how to handle the complex disbursement of funds (especially for renovations), and outlines what your relationship with the lender looks like after the deal closes.

## I. The Closing Process and Documentation

The closing process transforms a credit decision into a legal obligation. It protects three parties: you (by ensuring you get what you pay for), the lender (by securing their collateral), and the SBA (by ensuring program compliance).

We will look at this through the eyes of our two examples:

- Raj: A first-time buyer purchasing a 40-room independent motel for $1.8M. The motel was built in 1965.
- Anil: An experienced operator refinancing and renovating a 55-room motel into a Choice Hotels franchise with a $600K Property Improvement Plan (PIP).

### A. Finalizing Note Terms and the "Prepayment Trap"

The document you signed to get approved was likely a commitment letter. That is not the loan. The actual loan is governed by the **Promissory Note** and the **Loan Agreement**.

The Promissory Note is the legal instrument where you promise to pay back the money. Under SBA rules, this note must contain specific language.

1. Mandatory Note Terms

The Lender cannot write whatever they want. The Note must clearly state specific terms mandated by the SBA:

- The Interest Rate: Is it fixed or variable? If it is variable, it is likely tied to the Prime Rate plus a spread (e.g., Prime + 2.0%). The Note must state how often this adjusts (usually calendar quarterly or monthly).
- Maturity Date: For real estate loans like Raj's and Anil's, this is typically 25 years. For loans strictly for equipment or working capital not involving real estate, it is usually 10 years.
- Repayment Terms: This outlines your monthly payment.
- State-Specific Language: Every state has different laws about foreclosure and collateral. The SBA requires the lender to use the correct legal language for your specific state.

2. The Subsidy Recoupment Fee (Prepayment Penalty)

This is one of the most misunderstood aspects of SBA real estate loans. You might believe SBA loans have "no prepayment penalties." That is only true for loans under 15 years.

For loans with a maturity of 15 years or longer (like Raj's 25-year motel loan), the SBA enforces a **Subsidy Recoupment Fee**.

**Why This Matters:**

The SBA does not want borrowers using the program as a short-term bridge loan. They want to encourage long-term financing. If you prepay the loan early, the SBA wants to recoup the administrative costs (subsidy) they spent setting up your guarantee.

**The Rule (5% / 3% / 1%):**
If you voluntarily prepay more than 25% of the outstanding principal balance in the first three years, you owe a fee to the SBA:

- Year 1: 5% of the prepayment amount.
- Year 2: 3% of the prepayment amount.
- Year 3: 1% of the prepayment amount.
- Year 4+: No fee.

**Scenario: Raj's Refinance Mistake**
Raj buys his motel for $1.8M. Two years later, interest rates drop significantly. Raj decides to refinance his SBA loan with a conventional bank loan to save money on interest.

- He pays off the entire $1.8M balance in Year 2.
- The Penalty: He must pay a 3% fee on the prepayment.
- The Cost: $1.8M * 3% = $54,000.

Raj must write a check for $54,000 to exit the loan. When planning your exit strategy or future refinancing, you must account for this three-year lock-in period.

3. Separate Loan Agreements
The SBA does not strictly require a separate "Loan Agreement" document if the Promissory Note covers everything. However, most lenders use one anyway.

- The Rule: If a lender uses a separate Loan Agreement for their non-SBA commercial loans of similar size, they must use one for your SBA loan.
- Why This Matters: The Loan Agreement usually contains the "covenants." These are the ongoing rules you must follow, such as maintaining a certain Debt Service Coverage Ratio (DSCR). We will discuss these in detail in Part III.

## B. Borrower Certifications:

What You Are Swearing To before the lender releases the funds, you and your Operating Company (OC) must sign a series of certifications. These are not formalities. You are legally swearing to the federal government that specific facts are true. Lying on these forms is a federal crime.

No Adverse Change

You must certify that your financial condition has not significantly worsened since you applied.

- Scenario: Between approval and closing, a major storm damaged the roof of the motel Raj is buying. Revenue dropped 30% for two months.
- Requirement: Raj must disclose this. If he signs the form saying "no adverse change" while knowing the revenue has collapsed, he is committing fraud.
- Reality Check: If your revenue dips slightly, talk to your lender now. If you hide it and they find out later (via tax returns), they can call the loan.

2. Child Support Certification

This might surprise you. You must certify that no principal who owns 50% or more of the business is more than 60 days delinquent on child support payments.

- The Rule: If you are subject to an administrative order or court order for child support and are behind by more than 60 days, the loan cannot close until you bring it current.

"American-Made" Preference

The SBA requires a certification that, to the extent practicable, you will purchase American-made equipment and products with the loan proceeds. While this is a "preference" than a hard mandate, you must certify that you are making an effort to comply.

4. Illegal Activity and Tenant Restrictions

You must certify that the property will not be leased to or occupied by any business engaged in illegal activity.

- Cannabis: Under federal law, marijuana is illegal. You cannot lease space in your shopping center or hotel to a marijuana dispensary, even if it is legal in your state. You also cannot lease to a business that "supports" or "facilitates" illegal activity.

## C. Equity Injection Verification

This is the single most common reason for closing delays.

You promised to put money into the deal. Raj is putting in $180,000 (10% of the $1.8M purchase price). The lender cannot take Raj's word that he wrote a check. The SBA requires a forensic trail of that money.

1. The Requirement

The lender must verify your equity injection **prior** to disbursing a single dollar of the loan.

2. The Paper Trail (Source and Seasoning)

A check or a "gift letter" is not enough. The lender needs to see the life story of that money.

- Copy of the Check or Wire: Proof you sent the money to the closing agent.
- Source of Funds (Two Months): You must provide bank statements for the account the money came from, covering at least two full months (60 days) prior to the transfer.

- Evidence of Deposit: A settlement statement (often called a HUD-1) or an escrow receipt showing the money arrived at the closing agent's account.

**3. The "Borrowed Equity" Prohibition**

You generally cannot borrow your down payment. The equity must be *your* cash.

- The Exception: You can borrow the money if you have another source of income (outside the business you are buying) to repay that new debt.
- Example: Raj takes a Home Equity Line of Credit (HELOC) on his house to pay the $180,000. This is allowed *only if* Raj's wife has a salary from a separate job that can service the HELOC payments. If the repayment of the HELOC relies on the motel's profits, the SBA will reject it.

4. The "Sourcing" Trap

**Raj's Scenario:**

Raj has $180,000 to contribute.

- $100,000 is in his savings account. He has had it there for years. This is easy. He shows the bank statement.
- $80,000 was transferred from his brother last week.

**The Problem:** The lender sees a large deposit of $80,000 in Raj's account two weeks ago. They cannot count this as equity until they know where it came from.

- The Fix: Raj's brother must provide a "Gift Letter" stating the money is a gift, not a loan, and he does not expect repayment.
- The Extra Step: The lender might ask for *the brother's* bank statement to prove the brother didn't borrow the money to give to Raj.

**Pro Tip:** Do not move money between accounts during the

60 days before closing. Leave your down payment in one account and let it "season." Every time you move money, you create a new requirement for a paper trail.

## D. Insurance Requirements

You cannot close without specific insurance coverage. Lenders are rigid here because the SOP dictates exactly what they must get.

- Hazard Insurance: Must cover the full replacement cost of the building and contents. The policy must contain a "Mortgagee Clause" listing the lender.
- Liability Insurance: Protects against lawsuits (slip and fall).
- Flood Insurance: If the property is in a flood zone (even a low-risk one), this is federally mandated. No flood insurance, no loan.
- Life Insurance: The lender may require an assignment of life insurance on the key owner (Raj or Anil).

* *Why:* This protects the lender if the owner dies.

* *The Trap:* Getting a new life insurance policy requires medical exams and underwriting. This can take 4-6 weeks. If you wait until the week of closing to apply, your loan will be delayed.

* *Collateral Assignment:* You are not making the bank the "beneficiary." You are providing a "Collateral Assignment." This means the bank only gets paid the amount you owe on the loan; the rest goes to your family.

## E. Environmental Indemnification

Every SBA loan involving real estate requires an **Environmental Indemnification Agreement**.

By signing this, you agree to indemnify (hold harmless) the SBA and the lender against any liability for environmental contamination on the property. This applies even if you didn't cause the contamination.

- Scenario: Raj buys a motel. Five years later, the EPA finds that a dry cleaner next door leaked chemicals into the motel's groundwater 20 years ago.
- The Result: Raj is responsible for the cleanup costs. The Indemnification Agreement ensures the SBA is not left holding the bag for millions of dollars in EPA fines.

## II. Real Estate and Appraisals

For hotel buyers like Raj and Anil, the real estate is the primary collateral. The closing cannot happen until the value is confirmed.

### A. Appraisal Rules and Validity

Appraisals have a shelf life. The SBA requires the appraisal to be dated within 12 months of the application. If your closing drags on for a year (which happens in complex construction deals), you might need a new appraisal or a "recertification of value."

### B. The "Closing Value" Gap: PLP vs. Standard

The lender approved your loan based on an *estimated* value. Now, the appraiser gives the *actual* value.

**Scenario:** Raj is buying the motel for $1.8M. He needs the appraisal to come in at $1.8M.

- Outcome A: Appraisal is $1.85M. Great. No issues.
- Outcome B: Appraisal is $1.7M.

This is where the type of lender matters.

- Standard (Non-Delegated) Lender: If the appraisal is less than 90% of the estimated value ($1.62M in this case), the lender generally cannot close the loan without getting written permission from the SBA. This stops the process cold while they write a justification letter to the SBA center.

- PLP (Delegated) Lender: PLP lenders have more authority. If the appraisal is low, a PLP lender can document their own file with a justification (e.g., "The buyer is putting in extra equity to cover the gap") and proceed to closing without waiting for SBA permission.

**Why This Matters:** Knowing if your lender is a PLP lender helps you predict how fast they can solve an appraisal problem.

## C. The Historic Property Hurdle (Section 106)

Raj is buying a motel built in 1965. It looks like a standard roadside motor inn. He plans to renovate the lobby. He assumes this is simple.

He might be wrong.

1. The 50-Year Rule

The National Historic Preservation Act (Section 106) requires federal agencies to consider the impact of their projects on historic properties.

- The Trigger: Any property over 50 years old *might* be eligible for the National Register of Historic Places.
- The Review: Because the SBA is guaranteeing the loan, it counts as a federal project. The lender must determine if the property is historic.

2. SBA Form 2481

If Raj plans to renovate a property that is over 50 years old, the lender must conduct a review.

- No Renovation: If Raj is buying it and not touching the building, he signs SBA Form 2481 (Historic Property Borrower Certification). He certifies he will not alter, renovate, or demolish any part of the property.
- Renovation Planned: If Raj plans to remodel the lobby, and the building is deemed historically significant, the

SBA must consult with the State Historic Preservation Office (SHPO).

- The Delay: This consultation can take 30 days or more.
- The Risk: If Raj starts demolition *before* the SBA completes this review, the loan can be denied. Do not swing a hammer until you have clear written clearance from the lender about Section 106.

## III. Disbursement Management

Once all documents are signed, the lender is ready to release funds. This is called disbursement.

Disbursement works differently depending on whether you are buying a turnkey business or doing a renovation.

### A. General Disbursement Rules

1. The 48-Month Clock

The SBA wants projects to finish. The loan must be fully disbursed within 48 months of approval. If you have a massive construction project that stalls for four years, the SBA will cancel the remaining undisbursed balance.

2. SBA Form 1050 (Settlement Sheet)

This is the holy grail of disbursement. The Lender uses SBA Form 1050 to document exactly where every dollar went.

- Why it matters: The lender must prove that the loan proceeds were used for "eligible purposes." Buying the motel is eligible. Paying off your personal credit card debt is not.
- Evidence: For every check the lender cuts, they need an invoice or a settlement statement.

3. Joint Payee Checks

Often, the lender will not send money to you. They will send it to the people you owe.

- Example: The acquisition funds go to the Title Company/ Escrow Agent, not Raj.
- Example: If Anil buys furniture, the lender might write a check payable to "Anil's Motel LLC *and* Hotel Furniture Supply Corp." This ensures the vendor gets paid.

## B. Managing Construction and PIP (Property Improvement Plan)

This section is vital for Anil. He is buying a motel but also spending $600K to renovate it. Lenders handle renovation money with extreme caution. They fear "Mechanics' Liens."

**Definition:** A Mechanic's Lien is a legal claim filed by a contractor (plumber, electrician) who did work but didn't get paid. In many states, a Mechanic's Lien takes priority over the bank's mortgage. If the bank forecloses, they have to pay the plumber first. Banks hate this.

To prevent this, Anil faces a rigorous disbursement process for his $600K PIP.

1. The Construction Contract

Anil cannot hire "a guy" to fix the roof. The lender requires:

- A Fixed-Price Contract: A signed contract with a licensed general contractor. It must state a specific price.
- No Changes without Permission: Anil cannot decide halfway through to add a swimming pool without the lender's consent.
- Bonds: For large projects, the lender might require a "Payment and Performance Bond." This is insurance that pays to finish the job if the contractor goes bankrupt.

2. The Draw Process (How Anil gets paid)
Anil does not get a check for $600K at closing. The money is held in a "Construction Escrow" account.

- Step 1: The contractor completes the demolition and framing (e.g., $50,000 worth of work).
- Step 2: The contractor submits an invoice and a "Pay Application" to Anil.
- Step 3: Anil approves it and sends it to the lender.
- Step 4: The lender sends an inspector (which Anil pays for) to the job site. The inspector confirms the framing is done.
- Step 5: The lender releases the $50,000.

3. Lien Waivers
This is the most critical piece of paper in construction finance.

- The Rule: Before the lender releases payment 2, they require a Lien Waiver for payment 1.
- What it says: "I, the Contractor, certify that I have been paid $50,000 for the framing, and I waive my right to file a lien against the property for this portion of the work."
- Pro Tip: Anil needs to collect these from the General Contractor *and* the major subcontractors. If the General Contractor gets paid but doesn't pay the electrician, the electrician can still file a lien.

4. The "Do-It-Yourself" Prohibition
Anil is handy. He wants to save $20,000 by painting the rooms himself. He asks the lender if he can pay himself for the labor out of the loan proceeds.

**The Answer:** No.

- SBA Rule: Borrowers cannot be reimbursed for their own labor.

- Exceptions: The only exception is if Anil owns a separate, licensed construction company that acts as the contractor. Even then, that company cannot make a profit on the work. They can only bill for actual costs (materials and labor paid to employees).
- Funds Control: If Anil acts as his own contractor (owner-builder), the lender will almost certainly hire a third-party "Funds Control" firm to manage every invoice and check. This is expensive and administratively heavy.
- Recommendation: Hire an unaffiliated general contractor. It is cleaner, faster, and keeps the lender happy.

## IV. Post-Closing Loan Management

You survived closing. The money is disbursed. You are operating. Now you enter the "Servicing" phase.

You might think, "As long as I make my monthly payment, the bank will leave me alone." This is incorrect. Commercial loans have covenants and reporting requirements.

### A. Escrow for Taxes and Insurance

Like a home mortgage, the lender usually wants to ensure taxes and insurance are paid. If you don't pay property taxes, the county can seize the hotel. That wipes out the lender's collateral.

1. The Escrow Account

The lender will likely add a portion of the estimated annual taxes and insurance to your monthly loan payment.

- Cap on Collections: The SBA has a rule to prevent lenders from hoarding your cash. The lender cannot collect more than 105% of the estimated annual bill.

- Interest: If the account holds a significant balance, the lender must pay you interest on those funds if state law requires it for conventional loans.

Pro Tip: Review your escrow analysis annually. If property taxes drop (you appealed your assessment), make sure the lender lowers your monthly escrow payment.

## B. Financial Reporting Requirements

You are effectively partners with the bank. They have a right to know how the business is doing.

1. Annual Financial Statements

You must provide your business tax returns and financial statements (Profit & Loss, Balance Sheet) every year.

- Deadline: Usually within 90-120 days of the fiscal year-end.
- Why: The lender needs to calculate your Debt Service Coverage Ratio (DSCR) to grade the "risk" of the loan in their portfolio.

2. Interim Statements

For tighter deals or seasonal businesses (like hotels), the lender might demand quarterly or even monthly statements.

3. The "Adverse Change" Clause

Your loan agreement likely says you must notify the lender of any "material adverse change."

- Example: A major fire closes half of Raj's rooms.
- Example: Anil loses his franchise flag because he failed a quality inspection.
- Action: You must notify the lender. If you don't, and they find out later, it is a "non-monetary default."

### C. Covenants

Covenants are promises. There are two types: affirmative (things you must do) and negative (things you must not do).

1. The DSCR Covenant

This is the big one. Your loan agreement likely states: "Borrower must maintain a Debt Service Coverage Ratio of at least 1.25x."

- The Calculation: (Net Operating Income) / (Total Debt Service).
- What happens if you fail? If Raj has a bad year and his DSCR drops to 1.0x (he made enough to pay the bank, but no buffer), he is technically in default.
- The Reality: Banks rarely foreclose *solely* for a DSCR violation if payments are being made. However, it gives them use. They might freeze your ability to take owner distributions or increase your reporting frequency until the ratio improves.

2. Limitations on Distributions

Scenario: Anil has a great year. He wants to take $100,000 out of the company to purchase a personal vacation home.

- Check the Loan Agreement: Most SBA loan agreements prohibit distributions to owners *unless* the company remains compliant with all covenants (like the DSCR) after the money is taken out.
- The Risk: If Anil takes the money, and then the next quarter the business runs out of cash, the lender will look back at that distribution as a violation.

3. Limitations on more Debt

Raj cannot go out and take a second mortgage or a high-interest "merchant cash advance" (MCA) without the lender's permission.

- Why: An MCA lender takes payments daily from revenue. This hurts Raj's ability to pay the SBA loan.
- Consequence: Taking unauthorized debt is a major default.

## D. Post-Approval Modifications (327 Actions)

Life happens. Sometimes you need to change the terms of the loan *after* it is approved or even after it closes. In SBA language, this is often called a "327 Action" (named after the historical regulation code).

**Common Scenarios:**

- Changing Collateral: You want to sell a piece of equipment that is listed as collateral and replace it with a newer one.
- Releasing a Guarantor: You and your business partner are divorcing. You want to remove your ex-spouse as a guarantor.
- Changing Legal Structure: You want to move the business from an LLC to a Corporation.

**The Process:**

This is not as simple as the banker saying "sure."

- Lender Approval: The lender must analyze the request. (Does releasing the guarantor increase their risk? Is the new equipment e
- qual in value?)
- SBA Notification/Approval: Depending on the lender's status (PLP vs. Standard), they may need to send a formal request to the SBA service center.
- Timing: Do not expect this to happen overnight. A guarantor release or collateral substitution involves legal

amendments to the loan documents. Give your lender months of notice, not days.

### E. The Secondary Market Factor

One hidden aspect of SBA loans is the **Secondary Market**.

Lenders often sell the "guaranteed portion" (the 75% backed by the government) to investors. This is how they get their capital back to lend to the next borrower.

**Why this matters to you:**

If your loan is sold on the secondary market, the investor in New York or Chicago now technically owns the majority of your note.

- Inflexibility: If you call your local banker and ask to skip a payment or change your due date from the 1st to the 15th, they might say, "I can't do that."
- Why: They have to get permission from the investor who bought the loan. Investors buy these loans for a predictable cash flow. They generally do not like changes.
- Prepayment: As mentioned in Part I, the secondary market is the primary driver for the strict prepayment penalties. The investor paid a premium for your loan and expects it to last.

## V. Special Loan Structures: CAPLines

While Raj and Anil primarily used 7(a) term loans for real estate, they should be aware of the **Working Capital CAPLine**. This is a revolving line of credit.

### A. Borrowing Base Certificates (BBC)

Unlike a term loan where you get all the money at once, a CAPLine fluctuates based on your assets.

- The Mechanism: You can borrow up to a percentage of your Accounts Receivable (usually 80%) and Inventory (usually 50%).
- The Reporting: You must submit a Borrowing Base Certificate monthly. This report lists your current receivables and inventory.
- The Grind: If you stop sending the report, the lender freezes the line. You must stay disciplined with your bookkeeping.

### B. Seasonal CAPLines and the "Clean Up"

If Raj needs money for the summer tourist season, he might use a Seasonal CAPLine.

- The Clean Up Period: This line of credit is designed for *temporary* spikes. It is not for permanent working capital.
- The Rule: The SBA requires that you pay the balance down to zero for a period of at least 30 consecutive days each year.
- Why: This proves to the lender that the business is truly seasonal and can self-sustain during the off-season without the debt. If you cannot clean up the line, it means you have a structural cash flow problem, not a seasonal one.

## VI. Post-Closing Checklist for the Borrower

Here is what you need to do now after the funds land in your account.

- Review the Settlement Statement: Ensure the fees charged matched what you expected.
- Set up Auto-Pay: Most lenders require automatic debit (ACH) for payments. Ensure the account is funded.

- Calendar Reporting Dates: Put a recurring reminder in your calendar for tax return submission deadlines (usually April 15 or October 15).
- Keep Construction Records: If you are doing a PIP, buy a binder. Keep every invoice, every lien waiver, and every email. You will need them for the next draw.
- Review Insurance Expirations: Do not let your policy lapse. The lender will receive a notice now and will "force place" insurance, which is incredibly expensive.
- Locate Original Construction Dates: Check if your property is over 50 years old to anticipate Historic Property reviews for future renovations.

## VII. Reality Check: The Relationship Changes

Before closing, the lender was trying to win your business. After closing, they are managing risk.

If you hit a rough patch—a bad season, a road closure, a pandemic—communication is your best defense. The worst thing you can do is go silent. If you call the lender *before* you miss a payment, they have tools to help (deferments, interest-only periods). If you call them *after* the payment bounces, you are a collection account.

Manage the paperwork, respect the covenants, and keep the lines of communication open. That is how you turn a loan approval into a successful 25-year business asset.

### Next Steps

- Action: Ask your lender *now* if your loan will include the Subsidy Recoupment Fee language so you can plan your exit strategy.
- Action: If you have a renovation component, interview a CPA or bookkeeper who understands "construction

accounting" to help you manage the draw requests and lien waivers.

- Action: Review your personal cash reserves. Do you have enough to cover the first 3 months of loan payments if the business starts slow?
- Action: Verify if your property is over 50 years old. If so, ask your lender about the Section 106 review process before you sign any renovation contracts.

The mechanics are in place. You've closed, you're operating, and you understand your ongoing obligations. But before you go, there's one more chapter worth reading: the lessons learned from deals that succeeded and deals that failed. These patterns will help you avoid the traps that catch other hotel buyers.

CHAPTER 10

# SS
# LESSONS LEARNED

Having covered the entire loan lifecycle, here's the truth that separates winners from losers in hotel acquisitions: the biggest mistake isn't in the numbers or the paperwork—it's in the decisions nobody warned you about. Every successful hotel buyer you meet started exactly where you are now.

## I. Introduction: The Three-Headed Asset

The hospitality industry is a distinct animal in the sector of commercial lending. Unlike a dental practice or a manufacturing plant, a hotel is a hybrid asset. It is a piece of commercial real estate, an active operating business, and a collection of rapidly depreciating assets (furniture, fixtures, and equipment) all wrapped into one high-risk, high-reward package. Because of this complexity, hotel loans are scrutinized more heavily than almost any other industry sector.

Lenders view hotels as "special purpose properties." This legal definition matters significantly. If a dentist fails, the bank can sell the office building to an accountant or a lawyer. If a hotel fails, the bank can only sell it to another hotelier. The pool of buyers is smaller, and the risk of the asset losing value during a shutdown is catastrophic. A closed hotel starts smelling like mildew within a week; a closed office building gathers dust.

Throughout this guide, we have followed Raj and Anil through every stage of the SBA lending process. Now, as we consolidate the lessons learned, let us review where each borrower stands and the critical factors that will determine their success.

**Raj (The Independent Acquisition)**

Raj's $1.8 million motel purchase with 10% equity ($180,000) represents the classic first-time buyer scenario. His success depends on proving his management experience translates to ownership and maintaining post-closing liquidity.

**Anil (The Flag Conversion)**

Anil's $2.5 million project—including a $600,000 PIP to convert to Choice Hotels—represents the experienced operator expansion. His success depends on managing the global cash flow across his portfolio and executing the renovation on time and on budget.

This chapter synthesizes the technical requirements of the SBA's Standard Operating Procedure (SOP 50 10 8) with the practical realities Raj and Anil face. We will examine why loans like these get denied and how to structure them for approval.

## II. The Eligibility Minefield: Deal Killers

Before we look at financials or appraisals, we must clear the eligibility hurdles. Hotel loans have a high decline rate, often because the deal structure violates specific SBA credit standards about who can own and operate the business.

### A. The Citizenship Requirement (The 100% Rule)

For years, there was a misconception that if 51% of the business was owned by U.S. citizens, the loan was eligible. This is no longer true and is a frequent cause of denial for immigrant investment groups.

The Rule (PN 5000-876441, effective March 1, 2026):

The SBA requires that 100% of the direct and indirect ownership of the business be held by U.S. Citizens or U.S. Nationals with Principal Residence in the United States. Note: Lawful Permanent Residents (Green Card holders) are no longer eligible as of March 1, 2026.

There are no exceptions. The previous 5% de minimis rule was eliminated effective March 1, 2026. Any foreign ownership makes the loan ineligible.

**Case Application:**
Raj has an uncle in India who wants to invest $50,000 in exchange for 10% ownership.

- The Denial: If Raj accepts this money and gives his uncle 10% of the stock, the loan is ineligible. Any foreign ownership-even 1%-makes the deal ineligible as of March 1, 2026.
- The Fix: Raj's uncle cannot be an owner. He could potentially gift the money to Raj (if it is a true gift with no repayment expected), but he cannot hold equity on the cap table.

**Why This Matters:**
The SBA is a U.S. taxpayer-subsidized program designed to support the domestic economy. The regulations are strict to prevent U.S. government guarantees from benefiting foreign investors who do not reside here. You must verify the citizenship status of every person on your capitalization table before you sign a Letter of Intent.

### B. Passive vs. Active Operations (The Management Trap)

SBA loans are for "operating businesses," not passive real estate investments. You cannot simply buy a hotel and let someone else run it while you collect checks. This distinction is enforced through the review of the Management Agreement.

**The Rule:**
The borrower (Operating Company) must actively manage the hotel. If you hire a third-party management company, they must function as your *agent*, not your principal.

**The Trap:**
You might be tempted to sign standard management contracts that give the management company total control over hiring, firing, bank accounts, and check-signing authority.

**Case Application:**
Anil is busy with his other two hotels. He wants to hire a professional management company to run the new project. He signs a contract giving the management company full authority over the operating account and the right to set daily room rates without his approval.

- The Risk: The SBA may view Anil as a passive investor (a landlord) than a business owner. This makes the entity an Ineligible Passive Company (IPC).
- The Resolution: The management agreement must be reviewed by the lender and likely amended. The agreement must state that Anil retains ultimate control over the bank accounts, budgets, and policy decisions. The management company must report to him. If the management company employs the staff, Anil must still have the final say on the General Manager.

## C. Affiliation and Global Cash Flow

Hotels are rarely owned in isolation. Operators like Anil usually own multiple properties in different LLCs. The SBA views this web of companies as a single economic unit through the concept of **Affiliation**.

**The Rule (SOP Section A, Ch 1):**
If Anil owns 50% or more of Hotel A, and 50% or more of Hotel B, the SBA considers them "affiliates." When underwriting the new loan for Hotel C, the lender must verify that Hotel A and Hotel B are financially healthy.

**The Trap:**
One bleeding asset can kill a healthy acquisition.

**Case Application:**

- New Project (Hotel C): Projected DSCR 1.40 (Strong).
- Existing Hotel A: DSCR 1.25 (Stable).
- Existing Hotel B: DSCR 0.85 (Losing money due to local road construction).
- The Denial: When the lender calculates the "Global Cash Flow," the losses from Hotel B drag the average below 1.15. The lender fears Anil will siphon profits from the new SBA loan to subsidize the failing Hotel B.

**The Fix:**
Anil must address Hotel B before applying.

- Refinance: Can he lower the debt service on Hotel B?
- Explain: Can he prove the losses were one-time events (non-recurring) that are now over?
- Divest: In extreme cases, he may need to sell Hotel B to qualify for the loan on Hotel C.

## III. The Independent Path: Raj's Acquisition

Let us examine the specific hurdles Raj faces buying the unbranded, independent motel. His path is defined by "As-Is" valuation and the difficulty of proving future performance on a property with poor historical records.

### A. The "As-Is" Valuation Problem

Raj is buying the business for $1.8 million. The lender will order a commercial appraisal.

**The Valuation Gap:**

Independent motels often trade on "potential," but appraisers value based on "history." If the seller was running the business poorly (or hiding income), the income approach to value will be low.

- Scenario: The seller shows tax returns with zero profit. He tells Raj, "I take cash out, the real profit is $200,000."
- The Appraisal: The appraiser cannot value "under the table" cash. The appraisal comes back at $1.5 million based on the tax returns.
- The Gap: There is a $300,000 shortfall between the price ($1.8M) and the value ($1.5M).

**SBA Loan-to-Value (LTV) Limits:**

The SBA lender will generally base the loan amount on the *lower* of the purchase price or the appraised value. They cannot lend on "blue sky" or goodwill that isn't supported by cash flow.

**Raj's Options:**

1. Renegotiate: He must convince the seller that the business is only worth $1.5 million because the tax returns prove nothing else.
2. Seller Carry: The seller can carry the $300,000 difference

as a second note. However, this debt counts against Raj's DSCR unless it is on full standby (no payments) for the life of the loan.

## B. Special Purpose Collateral & Goodwill

Hotels are defined as **Special Purpose Properties** (SOP Section C, Ch 1). This designation has massive implications for collateral.

**The Three-Headed Asset:**

When a lender takes a hotel as collateral, they are taking three distinct asset classes:

- Real Property: The land and the building.
- Personal Property (Chattel): The beds, TVs, kitchen equipment, and reservation computers.
- Going Concern Value (Intangible): The business value, brand reputation, and goodwill.

**The Collateral Shortfall:**

Lenders are required to discount collateral values for liquidation analysis.

- Real Estate is often discounted to 85%.
- Chattel is often discounted to 50% or 10%.
- Goodwill is discounted to 0%.

If Raj pays $1.8 million, and the appraisal says $600,000 of that value is "Goodwill" (business value), the lender only has $1.2 million in tangible collateral. The SBA requires the lender to be "fully secured" if possible.

**Consequence:**

Because of this "collateral shortfall," the lender will likely require Raj to pledge more collateral. This usually means a lien on his personal residence or other investment properties. Raj needs to be prepared for this conversation. He is not betting the hotel; he is betting his house.

## C. Historic Property Review (Section 106)

Raj's motel was built in 1955. It has a classic mid-century look. While charming, this triggers a federal regulatory review under the National Historic Preservation Act.

**The Rule (SOP Section A, Ch 5):**
For any property over 50 years old, the lender must determine if it is listed on, or *eligible for listing* on, the National Register of Historic Places.

**The Action:**
Raj must sign **SBA Form 2481 (Historic Property Borrower Certification)**.

- *The Promise:* Raj certifies he will not alter the exterior of the building, demolish it, or do major earthmoving.
- *The Trap:* If Raj plans to tear down the old neon sign, change the roofline, or replace the windows with modern vinyl ones, he cannot sign this form.
- *The Consequence:* If he plans exterior renovations, the lender must initiate a "Section 106 Review" with the State Historic Preservation Office (SHPO). This involves hiring a historic consultant and waiting 30 to 90 days for the state to approve the renovation plans.
- *Advice:* For a first deal, avoid structural changes to historic properties unless you have significant time and capital. Stick to interior renovations (painting, carpets, furniture), which are usually exempt from Section 106 review.

## IV. The Flag Conversion: Anil's Expansion

Anil's project is more complex. He is buying a run-down asset to convert it into a franchise. This involves construction, projections, and strict brand compliance.

### A. The Property Improvement Plan (PIP)

A PIP is a punch list of renovations required by a brand (like Choice, Wyndham, or Marriott) to grant a franchise flag. It includes everything from new mattresses to lobby reconstruction and exterior signage.

**1. "Substantial" Renovation Rules:**

Because Anil is spending $600,000 on renovations (which is 30% of the purchase price), this is considered a significant construction project.

- "As-Completed" Appraisal: Anil needs the appraiser to value the hotel based on what it *will* be worth after the $600,000 is spent. He must provide the appraiser with the full PIP list and a contractor's fixed-price bid.
- The Upside: Hopefully, the "As-Completed" value comes in at $3.0 million. This gives Anil instant equity on paper and justifies the loan amount.

**2. The Contingency Fund:**

Renovations on old hotels always uncover surprises (mold behind the wallpaper, bad wiring). The SBA lender will require a **contingency reserve** (usually 10% of the construction budget) to be built into the loan proceeds.

- *Anil's Numbers:* $600,000 renovation + $60,000 contingency = $660,000 construction budget. Anil must ensure his loan request covers this, or he will have to pay the overages out of pocket.

## B. Managing Construction Draws

The bank does not hand Anil a check for $660,000 at closing. The money is placed in a restricted construction escrow account.

**The Draw Process:**

- Work First: The contractor completes a phase of work (e.g., demolition and framing).
- Inspection: The lender sends a third-party inspector to the hotel to verify the work is done.
- Lien Waivers: Anil must collect "Lien Waivers" from the general contractor and the subcontractors. These legal documents state that the workers have been paid and promise not to place a mechanics' lien on the property.
- Disbursement: Once the inspection and waivers are received, the bank wires the funds to the contractor.

**Reality Check:**

This process is slow. It can take 10 to 15 days from the request to the wire transfer. Anil must manage his contractor's expectations so work does not stop while waiting for a check.

## C. The Franchise Directory & "Comfort Letter"

Anil cannot close the loan without the franchise agreement being finalized.

**The SBA Franchise Directory:**

The lender will check the brand (Choice Hotels) against the **SBA Franchise Directory**.

- *If Listed:* The process is smooth. The SBA has already reviewed the brand's legal documents.

- *If Not Listed:* The lender cannot fund the loan until the franchise documents are reviewed and approved by the SBA, which can take weeks.

**The Lender's Access Agreement:**
Formerly known as a "Comfort Letter," this is a contract between the Bank and the Franchisor. It gives the Bank the right to step in and operate the hotel under the brand if Anil defaults on the loan.

- *The Friction Point:* Sometimes franchisors refuse to sign the SBA's standard addendum. If the franchisor is stubborn, the deal dies. Major brands are usually accustomed to this, but boutique flags can be difficult. Anil should ensure the franchisor is willing to sign the standard Lender's Access Agreement early in the process.

## V. Financial Analysis: The Numbers Game

Whether you are Raj or Anil, the math must work. The SBA has specific formulas for calculating whether a business can afford a loan.

### A. Debt Service Coverage Ratio (DSCR)

The SBA requires a DSCR of at least 1.15. This means for every $1.00 of loan payment, the business must generate $1.15 in available cash flow.

**The Formula:**
`Net Operating Income + Depreciation + Interest + Amortization / Annual Debt Service`

**The Add-Back Battle:**
You might rely on "add-backs" to boost their income numbers. An add-back is an expense listed on the tax return that you claim is profit.

- *Acceptable Add-Backs:* Depreciation (non-cash), Interest (because you are refinancing), Owner's Salary (if the new owner will not take a salary initially), One-time repairs (e.g., replacing a roof).
- *Unacceptable Add-Backs:* "I paid my staff in cash so it's not on the books," "I expensed my family vacation," or "I ran personal meals through the business."
- The Hard Truth: You cannot use illegal or unverifiable income to qualify for a federal loan. If it isn't on the tax transcript, it doesn't exist.

## B. Projections and the STAR Report

For Anil's renovation project, historical tax returns are irrelevant because he is changing the business model. He must submit two years of month-by-month projections.

**Justifying the Numbers:**

Anil cannot simply guess that occupancy will be 70%. He needs data. The gold standard in the hotel industry is the STAR Report (STR).

- Competitive Set: The report compares Anil's hotel to 4-5 nearby competitors (e.g., Holiday Inn Express, Hampton Inn).
- Penetration Index: If the competitors are running at 75% occupancy with an Average Daily Rate (ADR) of $120, Anil can justify projecting his hotel at 70% occupancy and $115 ADR once renovated.
- Ramp-Up: The projections must be realistic. He should show 30% occupancy in Month 1, growing to stabilized occupancy by Month 12.

**Interest Reserve:**
Since cash flow will be negative during the renovation and ramp-up, Anil should ask for an **Interest Reserve**. This allows the loan proceeds to pay the loan interest for the first 6 to 12 months, preventing him from paying out of pocket while the hotel is under construction.

## C. Equity Injection: The Source and Path

The SBA 7(a) program allows for a 10% equity injection. This is remarkably low compared to conventional loans (which require 25-35%), but the verification is strict.

**1. The 10% Rule:**
For a change of ownership, you must inject at least 10% of the total project cost (Purchase Price + Renovation + Closing Costs).

**2. The Seller Note Limit:**
Can the seller lend you the down payment? Only partially.

- The Rule (SOP Section B, Ch 1): Seller debt on "full standby" (no payments for the life of the SBA loan) can count toward the equity injection, but only for half of the required amount.
- *Example:* If Raj needs $180,000 (10%) for equity, he *must* provide $90,000 (5%) of his own cash. The seller can carry a note for the other $90,000 (5%) on full standby. Raj cannot borrow the entire 10% from the seller.

**3. Sourcing and Seasoning:**
Lenders must verify the "Source and Path" of the funds.

- Seasoning: The money should ideally be in Raj's bank account for two months.
- The Paper Trail: If Raj moves money from a brokerage account to a savings account, he must provide statements

for *both* accounts showing the wire transfer. Lenders must prove the money did not come from a credit card or another undisclosed loan.

## VI. Environmental & Zoning Hurdles

Before the loan closes, the physical property must pass two major tests.

### A. Environmental Contamination (Phase I ESA)

Hotels are high-risk for environmental issues.

- The Laundry Problem: Older motels often had on-site dry cleaning machines that used perchloroethylene (perc), a hazardous chemical. If perc leaked into the soil, it creates a massive cleanup liability.
- The Process: A Phase I Environmental Site Assessment (ESA) is mandatory.
- The Risk: If the Phase I identifies a "Recognized Environmental Condition" (REC), a Phase II (soil and groundwater testing) is required. This costs $5,000-$15,000 and takes weeks.
- Pro Tip: Ask the seller for any prior environmental reports *before* you spend money on a new one.

### B. Zoning and Non-Conforming Use

Many older hotels (like Raj's 1955 motel) are "Non-Conforming." They were built legally in 1955, but zoning laws have changed. Maybe the motel is too close to the road (setback issues) or lacks enough parking spots by modern standards.

**The "Burn Down" Letter:**
The lender needs a letter from the municipality stating that if the hotel burns down (damage > 50%), it can be rebuilt exactly as it is today.

- The Danger: Some cities have ordinances saying that if a non-conforming property is destroyed, it must be rebuilt according to *current* code. If the current code requires a 50-foot setback and the lot is only 80 feet deep, you cannot rebuild the hotel. This makes the collateral worthless.
- The Fix: If the city refuses to issue a rebuild letter, the lender may require "Ordinance and Law" insurance coverage, which pays for the lost value if rebuilding is prohibited.

## VII. Success Patterns: How to Win

Based on hundreds of closed hotel loans, here are the patterns that lead to approval.

### The Story Matches the Numbers

If Raj claims he will increase revenue by 20%, his resume must show he knows marketing. If Anil claims he will save money on labor, his existing hotels must show low labor costs. Lenders look for consistency between the borrower's background and the financial projections.

### Post-Closing Liquidity

Lenders hate to see a borrower drain their last dollar to make the equity injection.

- The Target: Lenders want to see that after Raj pays his $180,000, he still has $20,000 to $50,000 in the bank for emergencies. If the equity injection zeroes out his account, the loan is viewed as distress-prone.

### Organized Documentation

The borrowers who close are the ones who have their documents ready. Using a checklist is not optional; it is mandatory for survival.

## VIII. The Ultimate Hotel Loan Checklists

To ensure a smooth process, Raj and Anil should use the following checklists. These are split into "Deal Killers" (check these first) and "Closing Docs" (check these later).

### A. The "Deal Killer" Checklist (Do This Before Applying)

- ☐ Citizenship: Are 100% of the owners U.S. Citizens or U.S. Nationals with Principal Residence in the U.S.? (No exceptions-Green Card holders no longer eligible as of March 1, 2026)
- ☐ Management: Will the borrower actively manage the business? If hiring a management company, is the contract structured as an agency agreement?
- ☐ Affiliation: Are all other hotels owned by the borrower financially healthy (DSCR > 1.0)?
- ☐ DSCR Check: Does the tax return (or projection) show a DSCR > 1.15?
- ☐ Equity Verification: Do you have the 5% minimum cash? Is the other 5% covered by a standby seller note?
- ☐ Environmental: Did the property ever have on-site dry cleaning?
- ☐ Zoning: Is the property legally non-conforming? Can it be rebuilt if destroyed?

### B. The Raj (Independent Buyer) Checklist

- ☐ Seller Financials: 3 years of Federal Tax Returns + Interim P&L (dated within 90 days).
- ☐ Management Resume: Detailed history of Raj's experience with specific metrics (managed 40 employees, budget of $2M).
- ☐ Business Plan: Specific to this property. "I will cut laundry costs by 15% by installing high-efficiency washers in Month 3."
- ☐ Historic Certification: SBA Form 2481 (if property is >50 years old).
- ☐ Entity Docs: Articles of Organization and Operating Agreement for the new LLC.

### C. The Anil (Flag Conversion) Checklist

- ☐ PIP List: The official document from the Franchisor detailing required work.
- ☐ Construction Budget: Fixed-price contractor bids matching the PIP line items.
- ☐ Franchise Agreement: Copy of the executed agreement or Letter of Intent.
- ☐ Lender's Access Agreement: Confirmation that the Franchisor will sign the SBA addendum.
- ☐ Projections: 2 years of month-by-month projections with assumptions (ADR, Occupancy) tied to a STAR Report.
- ☐ Global Debt Schedule: List of all debts/notes for Anil's other properties.

### D. Closing Documentation (The Final Hurdle)

- ☐ IRS Form 4506-C: Signed for tax transcript verification.
- ☐ Insurance: Hazard, Liability, Flood (if applicable), and Life Insurance assignment.

- ☐ Standby Agreements: If seller financing is used, the Note and Standby Agreement must be executed.
- ☐ Equity Injection Proof: Final wire transfer receipt and the bank statement showing the funds leaving the borrower's account.
- ☐ Lien Waivers: (For construction) Signed waivers from the general contractor.

## IX. Conclusion

Hotel lending is a marathon, not a sprint. The "Tales of Raj and Anil" illustrate that success is not about finding a good building; it is about structuring a compliant deal.

For Raj, the path to success lies in explaining his "diamond in the rough" strategy and proving that he can bridge the valuation gap with sweat equity and solid management. For Anil, success depends on managing the complexity of construction, ensuring his PIP budget is realistic, and proving that his expansion strengthens his portfolio than diluting it.

By understanding the "Why" behind the SBA's rules—why they insist on active management, why they scrutinize foreign ownership, and why they fear environmental risks—you stop fighting the process and start managing it. The borrowers who provide clear, organized documentation that addresses these fears upfront are the ones who get to the closing table.

**Next Steps:**

- Raj: Must sit down with the seller and get the exact tax returns. If they don't support the loan, he must renegotiate the price or walk away.
- Anil: Must get his contractor bids finalized to ensure the $600K budget is realistic before the appraisal is ordered.

The SBA hotel loan is the most powerful tool for wealth creation in the hospitality industry, provided you respect the complexity of the instrument.

**Sources:**

- SOP 50 10 8, Section A, Ch 1 (Eligibility & Affiliation)
- SOP 50 10 8, Section B, Ch 1 (Credit Standards & Equity)
- SOP 50 10 8, Section B, Ch 3 (Appraisals & Construction)
- SOP 50 10 8, Section A, Ch 5 (Historic Properties & Environmental)
- PN 5000-876441 (Citizenship Requirements, effective March 1, 2026 - rescinds PN 5000-872050)

# GLOSSARY OF HOTEL SBA TERMS

**ADR (Average Daily Rate):** Total room revenue divided by number of rooms sold. A key metric for hotel valuation and underwriting.

**Affiliation Rules:** SBA regulations that combine the financials of related businesses. If you own multiple hotels, lenders evaluate them together.

**Airball:** The portion of an SBA loan that exceeds available collateral value. Lenders and SBA share this unsecured risk.

**Amortization:** The schedule for paying down loan principal. SBA real estate loans typically offer 25-year amortization.

**CDC (Certified Development Company):** The nonprofit entity that provides the SBA portion of a 504 loan.

**Collateral:** Assets pledged to secure the loan. For hotels, this primarily means the real estate and FF&E.

**DSCR (Debt Service Coverage Ratio):** Net Operating Income divided by annual debt payments. Lenders typically require 1.15x to 1.25x minimum.

**Equity Injection:** The borrower's cash contribution to the project. Minimum 10% for most hotel transactions.

**FF&E (Furniture, Fixtures & Equipment):** Beds, TVs, lobby furniture, ice machines, shuttle vans, and similar items.

**Flag:** A hotel brand (Hilton, Marriott, Choice, Wyndham, etc.). Flagged hotels operate under franchise agreements.

**Franchise Agreement:** The contract between a hotel owner and a brand. Governs standards, fees, term, and termination rights.

**Goodwill:** The intangible value of a business above its hard assets. Includes reputation and going-concern value.

Guarantee Fee: The upfront fee paid to SBA for their loan guarantee. As of FY 2025: 0% for loans up to $1M; 3.5% on the guaranteed portion up to $1M plus 3.75% on amounts over $1M for larger loans.

**Independent:** A hotel operating without a national brand affiliation.

LPR (Lawful Permanent Resident): Green card holder. Note: As of March 1, 2026 (PN 5000-876441), LPRs are NO LONGER ELIGIBLE for SBA loan guarantees. Only U.S. Citizens and U.S. Nationals with Principal Residence in the U.S. may own SBA-financed businesses.

**Management Agreement:** Contract with a third-party company to operate the hotel.

**NOI (Net Operating Income):** Revenue minus operating expenses, before debt service.

**Occupancy Rate:** Rooms sold divided by rooms available. Expressed as a percentage.

**PIP (Property Improvement Plan):** Required renovations specified by a franchisor as condition of granting or renewing a franchise.

**Phase I ESA:** Environmental Site Assessment. Required for all SBA real estate loans.

**RevPAR (Revenue Per Available Room):** Total room revenue divided by total rooms available.

**SBA 504 Loan:** Program combining bank financing (50%), CDC financing (40%), and borrower equity (10%).

Tip: 504 loans cannot cover working capital or franchise fees. However, borrowers can get a separate 7(a) loan for these purposes alongside a 504. The $5.0 million 7(a) maximum applies independently.

**SBA 7(a) Loan:** The SBA's primary loan program. Offers flexibility for acquisition, equipment, working capital, and construction.

**Seller Note:** Financing provided by the property seller. Must be on standby to count toward equity.

**SOP 50 10 8:** Standard Operating Procedures for SBA lending. The rulebook lenders must follow.

**STAR Report: STR (formerly STR, now CoStar) report comparing a hotel's performance to its competitive set.**

# RESOURCES FOR HOTEL BUYERS

## SBA Resources

SBA.gov: www.sba.gov — Official information on loan programs and lender search

SBA Lender Match: www.sba.gov/lendermatch — Connect with SBA-approved lenders

SBA District Offices: www.sba.gov/local-help — Local SBA representatives

**SBA Forms (Direct Download Links)**

Form 1919 (Borrower Information): www.sba.gov/document/sba-form-1919-borrower-information-form

Form 413 (Personal Financial Statement): www.sba.gov/document/sba-form-413-personal-financial-statement

Form 1919 (Statement of Personal History): www.sba.gov/document/sba-form-912-statement-personal-history

Form 4506-C (IRS Tax Transcript Request): Available from your lender or www.irs.gov

## Hotel Industry Resources

STR (formerly STR, now CoStar Group): www.str.com — STAR reports and benchmarking

AAHOA: www.aahoa.com — Asian American Hotel Owners Association

AHLA: www.ahla.com — American Hotel & Lodging Association

## Free Counseling

SCORE: www.score.org — Free mentoring from experienced business professionals

SBDC: www.sba.gov/sbdc — Free consulting and training nationwide

# QUICK REFERENCE CHECKLISTS

## Pre-Application Checklist

- ☐ All owners are U.S. Citizens or U.S. Nationals with Principal Residence in the U.S. (Green Card holders no longer eligible as of March 1, 2026)
- ☐ Business will be actively managed by borrower
- ☐ If using management company, agreement preserves borrower control
- ☐ Property does not have extended-stay rooms (30+ day average stays)
- ☐ You have 10% minimum equity injection available
- ☐ Any existing hotels you own are performing (DSCR > 1.0)
- ☐ You can get 3 years of seller's tax returns
- ☐ Property has no known environmental contamination

## Documentation Checklist: Personal

- ☐ Government-issued photo ID (all owners)
- ☐ Social Security cards (all owners)
- ☐ 3 years personal federal tax returns
- ☐ Personal Financial Statement (SBA Form 413)
- ☐ Resume detailing hospitality experience

## Documentation Checklist: Acquisition

- ☐ Signed Letter of Intent or Purchase Agreement
- ☐ Seller's 3 years federal tax returns
- ☐ Seller's year-to-date financials
- ☐ Inventory of FF&E being purchased
- ☐ Allocation of purchase price

# A FINAL WORD

The SBA hotel loan is the most powerful wealth-building tool available to independent hoteliers. It allows you to acquire properties with 10% down that would otherwise require 30-40% equity. It provides 25-year terms that maximize cash flow. It bundles real estate, equipment, goodwill, and working capital into a single financing package.

But this power comes with complexity.

The borrowers who succeed are those who understand the rules before they sign a purchase agreement. They structure deals that work within SBA guidelines than fighting the system. They provide complete documentation packages that answer lender questions before they are asked.

Raj and Anil represent thousands of hotel buyers who complete this process every year. Some are acquiring their first property after years of managing for others. Some are expanding portfolios they have built over decades. All share the same goal: building wealth through hotel ownership while managing risk intelligently.

This guide has given you the roadmap. The checklists, the timelines, the specific requirements for hotel transactions. Use them.

You now have both the ambition and the preparation.

Go get funded.

# ABOUT THE AUTHOR

Thomas Hartwell has spent years studying SBA lending programs and small business financing. His research includes SBA Standard Operating Procedures (SOP 50 10 8, effective June 2025), procedural notices, official forms, and current lender practices. Through extensive analysis of government policies and industry requirements, he has developed deep knowledge of what it takes for small business owners to successfully work through the loan process. His work focuses on translating complex federal programs and banking requirements into practical guidance for entrepreneurs. He is the author of the FUNDED series of SBA lending guides.

APPENDIX

# READER GUIDE

## About This Guide

This guide exists because hotel financing is different from every other type of small business loan.

When you purchase a retail store or a professional practice, lenders evaluate a relatively simple business model. When you purchase a hotel, you are purchasing a 24-hour operating business, a real estate asset, a brand relationship (if flagged), and a hospitality operation all wrapped into one transaction.

Most SBA guides treat hotels as an afterthought, lumping them in with "commercial real estate" or "hospitality businesses." They miss the specific challenges you face: Property Improvement Plans (PIPs) that can add $500,000 to your project cost. Franchise agreements that give brands unusual control over your business. Seasonality that makes your January cash flow look nothing like your July numbers. Management agreements that can disqualify your entire loan if structured incorrectly.

There is another challenge most guides never mention: bank capacity. Hotel loans count toward a bank's Commercial Real Estate (CRE) concentration. Federal regulators track these concentrations closely. When a bank's total CRE loans exceed 300% of its risk-based capital, regulators require enhanced oversight. Many banks self-limit their hotel lending well before hitting this threshold. You may approach a bank with a perfect deal and hear "We're not doing hotels right now." The bank is not rejecting you; it is managing its regulatory exposure. If you hear this, ask for a referral to another SBA lender, or work with a broker who knows which lenders have capacity.

This guide addresses those realities head-on.

This guide structures every chapter around the actual questions hotel buyers ask, and more importantly, around the questions they should be asking but often do not. Whether you are a first-time buyer looking at a 40-room highway motel or an experienced operator converting your third property to a national flag, you will find specific guidance for your situation.

The SBA loan programs covered here (primarily 7(a) and 504) represent the most powerful financing tools available to independent hoteliers. They offer lower down payments, longer terms, and more flexible structures than conventional commercial mortgages. But they come with rules that can trip up even experienced borrowers.

Understanding those rules before you make an offer on a property can save you months of frustration and thousands of dollars in wasted due diligence costs.

## Meet the Characters

Throughout this guide, you will follow two hotel buyers whose situations likely mirror your own:

### Raj: The First-Time Buyer

Raj spent fifteen years managing hotels for others. He started as a front desk clerk, worked his way up to General Manager, and has run properties ranging from 60-room limited-service hotels to 150-room full-service operations. He knows RevPAR, he knows labor scheduling, and he knows how to handle a 2 AM noise complaint.

Now he wants to own.

Raj has found a 40-room independent highway motel listed

at $1.8 million. The property is dated but solid. It needs cosmetic work, not structural repairs. The seller is an aging owner ready to retire.

Raj has $180,000 for equity injection (10% of purchase price). He has never handled SBA paperwork. He has never negotiated with a lender from the borrower's side of the table. His challenge is proving that his management experience translates into ownership capability, while structuring a deal that preserves enough cash for the inevitable surprises.

### Anil: The Expansion Play

Anil already owns two hotels. Both are profitable. Both were acquired with SBA financing. He understands the process.

Now he wants to acquire a 55-room independent motel and convert it to a Choice Hotels flag (Comfort Inn). The total project cost is $2.5 million: $1.9 million for acquisition plus $600,000 for the Property Improvement Plan (PIP) required by the franchisor.

Anil's challenge is different from Raj's. He must prove that adding a third property strengthens than strains his portfolio. He must coordinate between his lender, the SBA, the franchisor, and a general contractor. He must manage construction draws while keeping his existing properties running smoothly.

Their stories illustrate the range of hotel SBA transactions, from straightforward acquisitions to complex flag conversions with construction components.

## How to Use This Guide

If you are exploring SBA financing: Start with Chapter 1 to understand whether this path makes sense for your situation.

If you have a specific property in mind: Jump to Chapter 2 (eligibility) and Chapter 6 (underwriting) to assess whether your deal structure will work.

If you are already in the application process: Use Chapter 5 (documentation) and Chapter 10 (checklists) to ensure nothing falls through the cracks.

If you are working with a lender: Share the relevant sections with your loan officer. A borrower who understands the SBA's requirements makes the lender's job easier and speeds your approval.

Every chapter includes specific scenarios, practical checklists, and the reasoning behind SBA requirements. Understanding the "why" helps you structure deals that work the first time.

**Disclaimer**

This book provides general information based on SBA Standard Operating Procedure 50 10 8 and related regulations as of the publication date. SBA policies change regularly. Always verify current requirements with your lender and the SBA.

For updates and additional resources,
visit www.hartwelllabs.com.

www.ingramcontent.com/pod-product-compliance
Ingram Content Group UK Ltd.
Pitfield, Milton Keynes, MK11 3LW, UK
UKHW040232290926
15471UKWH00002B/154

9 798994 707913